LORD OF THE SECOND ADVENT

STEVE KEMPERMAN

Regal Books

A Division of GL Publications
Ventura, California, U.S.A.

The foreign language publishing of all Regal books is under the direction of GLINT. GLINT provides financial and technical help for the adaptation, translation and publishing of books for millions of people worldwide. For information regarding translation, contact: GLINT, P.O. Box 6688, Ventura, California 93006.

Some of the names have been changed in this book to protect their privacy.

Trade edition, 1982

Published by Regal Books
A Division of GL Publications
Ventura, California 93006
Printed in U.S.A.

Library of Congress Catalog Card No. 80-54091
ISBN 0-8307-0868-5

Contents

Dedication

This book is dedicated to my dear mother and father, Wilna and Joop Kemperman. Their great love and courage persisted through the long dark night of my cult imprisonment and finally helped bring in the dawn, helped me to begin life anew. All my words, all my gifts, and all my tears can never express my gratitude for what you have done for me. But we are together again, and I love you. And that is so very, very good.

Foreword

When beset by severe and unusual stress in society—war, famine, epidemic, economic dislocation, radical changes in social mores—people long for utopias: heavens on earth. Either sincerely in response to this longing or cunningly taking advantage of this longing, utopian cults appear with their strong, charismatic leaders. This is such a time.

Since World War II, at least 2,500 cults with 2 million—3 million members, have appeared on the American landscape. These cults use such sophisticated control mechanisms that their members find it almost impossible to break out of the psychological bondage imposed upon them.

While some smaller sex-and-drug cults appeal to the baser nature of their adherents, the larger cults appeal to the idealism of youth—a desire to know more about God, a desire to improve society. It was from this reservoir of idealistic youth that Steve Kemperman was drawn into the Unification Church.

I met Steve soon after he professed to renounce the cult. I saw him frequently read his Bible. He was attentive and questioning during discussions of contrasts between what the Bible teaches and what various cults teach. Steve is one of several millions who are regularly recruited and retained by cults through deception and thought-reform techniques. These idealistic young adults are conditioned to believe that God reveals Himself *only* through their particular messiah, guru, or Bible teacher, and to look with disdain on all religious institutions but their own. A few become disillusioned and are able to walk out of the cults, usually with devastating spiritual and psychological trauma during the following year or two. Others are assisted to freedom by parents who provide re-personalization counseling and aids for reentry into society, thus making the return to reality quicker and more effective.

Many fine organizations across our land through education and/ or action are laboring to multiply Steve Kemperman a thousandfold and hear the joyful shouts, "I'm Free! I'm Free!" May *your* family be so fortunate that it will not be affected by the cult movement.

George W. Swope
Department of Counseling and Student Development
Westchester Community College, Valhalla, New York

Acknowledgements

Many wonderful people helped in the realization and creation of this book. For their expert tutoring, literary advice, and support I am deeply indebted to William Wiser, teacher and novelist; D. Keith Mano, novelist, writer and friend; Richard Baltzell, wise and magnanimous editor with *Celestial Arts*; and my mentor and talented editor at the Residential College at the University of Michigan, Warren Hecht.

For extensive and valuable editing, I thank Dr. George Swope, Mr. and Mrs. J.H.B. Kemperman, and my brother Eric. I also thank Steve Hassan for his help as an invaluable information resource and for his effective advice and input during my stay at the Carriage House.

Before my mind could be freed from cult control, a few courageous souls had to risk their hides in a daring rescue attempt. My sincerest and deepest thanks to my father and mother, my brother Bruce Kemperman, Jan and Ada Trommel, Tom Trabka, Andrew Donavel, Frank Carrol and Jack Hall.

A very special and warm *thank you* goes to George and Winifred Swope. In the face of serious cult threats and financial disaster they possessed the moral conviction and courage to establish their home as a rehabilitation center for ex-cultists. Special thanks to Joy Shores for her competent and compassionate service as staff director of the Carriage House.

Finally, I am deeply thankful to all those who lent support to my parents or who in some way gave their time and effort in helping to realize my human freedom. Though I can't enumerate your many acts of generosity and human service, my appreciation for your contributions nevertheless flows strong and sincere: my brothers and one sister Ingrid; Paul Engel; Ellen Gallagher; Lorna and Bill Goldberg; Dr. Gail and Irene Young; Dr. Robert Boon; Dr. Burt Kay; Frank Blaakman; Shelly Turner; Jim C. Britt; Dr. John Harper; Dr. David Cox; Dr. May Ann Maher; Paula Keilson; Dr. Govind Mudholkar; Dr. Gerard Emch; Dr. Reuben Gabriel; Dave, Steve and Tom Vail; Nancy Smith; Andy Stubbs; Rick Dory; Jim Hoppin; and last but a million miles from least, Caroline Bowles.

Chapter One

Deprogramming!

*"I have sworn upon the altar of God
eternal hostility against every form
of tyranny over the mind of man,"*
Thomas Jefferson.

Justin and I tramped towards the security checkpoint where two guards were busy inspecting handbags and waving people through the metal-detector. It was Christmas morning, and the Richmond airport terminal looked like an anthill a small child had kicked open.

After two years in the Unification Church I'd come to hate my fund-raising life, to loathe the mindless pounding of America's streets day after weary day on only four hours sleep a night. Now I was headed for my family's home to four days of peace and rest. Temporary asylum. I stood next to my team captain and gazed over the crowd into oblivion, relishing the first moments of this rare vacation. Suddenly a guard was ushering me through the checkpoint. Justin and I shook hands.

"*Manseei*, Steve, Father be with you."

"Justin, you're a fantastic Abel. If anyone's going to bring victory for our True Parents this year it'll be you" (1976 was the year of the great campaigns when Father would speak at Yankee Stadium and Washington Monument). Justin chuckled and told me to get going. A minute later I pushed through a glass door into the chill air and blasting whine of jet engines. *Manseei* is a Korean term meaning "victory for ten thousand years." "Father" referred to both God and our True Father, Sun Myung Moon—Lord of the Second Advent, True Son of God, the Messiah.

From my window seat I saw only wet, grey-tin mist. Richmond was clammy-cold, with ice covering the sidewalks and streets. Although I was looking forward to the trip home as a break from the fund-raising grind, this fourth visit in two years was, more than ever, a journey into enemy territory. For one thing, Satan claimed everything outside the Unification Church, the whole mess, my parents included. And Mom and Dad's intense opposition to the Unification Family made this visit all the more spiritually threatening.

The last time I'd seen my folks, in the spring, we had spent the best part of my stay in sizzling debate. I'll never forget that one night in the living room with the whole family powwowed around. We argued passionately and through the wee hours about the *Divine Principle* (God's "revelation" to Sun Myung Moon and the Bible of the Unification Church), about all the money we raised, about Father's mansions and Lincoln Continentals, and about all that garbage concerning how we were brainwashed, our thinking limited and controlled by the group's indoctrination. Dad even had the gall to ask me to see a psychiatrist!

Every week several Brothers and Sisters were kidnapped by their parents and then deprogrammed. What was it that alarmed these parents so much that they would try to get their children out of the Church? If they could only understand that they were dealing with the True Family of God, the Messiah's Family!

For a Unification Church member, deprogramming is synonymous with spiritual death. Satan would suck you back into the fallen world, to living hell. A spiritual scar would brand the physical family and all its descendants for eternity. In a telephone conversation about a year ago Mom had mentioned that although they thought Father was a phony, they would never try to kidnap and deprogram me. Still, I worried at times. If they remained as opposed to the Family as they were now, perhaps someday they might in desperation go to any length to get me out.

Well, there was no use thinking about it. And I couldn't really imagine Mom and Dad doing such a thing. No matter what the spiritual climate at home, I was determined to be a shining example of the True Parents (Sun Myung Moon and his wife Hak Ja Han). I would smile a lot, act cheerful and impress the folks with my high standard of love and service. This might even lessen their negativity towards the Church. I also resolved to chant and pray regularly to guard against any kind of satanic invasion.

The plane taxied to a stop and passengers began to disembark. As I descended the steps and crunched over the runway towards the terminal I spotted Mom standing behind a frosty plate glass window. She was waving her hands over her head like an excited little girl. I had forgotten how beautiful she was, especially for a woman of 43. Both of my parents come from Holland and Mom looked very Dutch with her fair skin, light brown hair and eyes like azure stones.

Dad towered behind Mom in the crowd that pressed against the glass. The deep smile-wrinkles sprang around his eyes, the warm moist eyes of a father who loves his oldest son more than the son will ever know. Dad is Dutch to the core but doesn't fit the traditional image of the fair-skinned Dutchman. Actually, he looks more like a Spanish aristocrat with his deep tan skin and jet black hair speckled with strands of grey. He used to tell jokes about how a handsome Spanish soldier slipped into the family one romantic night during Spain's occupation of Holland in the sixteenth century. His shoulders were lumberjack-broad, his chest bulky and he stood a little over six-feet-one-inch. The Kemperman nose was wide and fleshy but didn't look unattractive with his strong jaw and high forehead.

Before I could put my luggage down Mom had wrapped her arms around my neck and kissed me on the cheeks. "Oh Sweetheart, it's so good to have you home." Then Dad squeezed me in a good old Dutch father-to-son kiss. I was always amazed by the warmth with which Dad greeted me on my rare visits. You'd think I was his only son coming home from the war. And I'd forgotten that Mom used to call me "Sweetheart." I had even forgotten the melody of their Dutch accents.

For a second I winced with shame and regret that I didn't love my parents nearly as much as they loved me. My love for Dad had diminished the most over the past two years since I'd joined the movement. Before, I had been immensely proud of my dad, the brilliant professor of mathematics, the incredibly learned scholar and dedicated father who would sell his soul to help his kids. Now he was just another spiritually dead egghead of the fallen world. My mother and father were just "physical parents." They led selfish, self-centered lives, contributing nothing to the restoration and salvation of the world. In a way it was too bad for Mom and Dad. But in time they too would come to know the Lord and His bride, and realize that Sun Myung Moon and Hak Sha Han really were my True Parents.

Not only had my feelings for my family changed, my physical appearance had also changed. The collar-length hair, dungarees and T-shirt had vanished. I looked more like a cadet coming home from his first semester at a military academy—hair cropped short, brown straight-legged slacks and matching penny-loafers, a light blue shirt with a scrawny collar. (I'd taken my tie off in the plane.)

My three younger brothers and little sister took turns hugging me and the whole family plopped down on chairs and sofas in a circle around the coffee table. That entire afternoon we sipped coffee, nibbled Dutch almond cookies, laughed, talked and took turns opening presents (a family tradition).

Shaggy, brown-haired Bruce slouched in the green sofa smoking a cigarette. His long frame was a good two inches over my six-feet-one-inch. He was 19 and a sophomore at the University of Colorado at Boulder. His worn, frayed jeans, faded brown khaki shirt and dingo boots conjured up a brief flashback of my former days.

Hubert, a senior at Brighton High, shifted about on the edge of the cream sofa and chatted nonstop. With his blond hair and blue eyes he looked like the little Dutch boy on the paint can. About a year before he'd become a Christian. Even though he was following Jesus Christ and not the true Messiah, I had to admit that he was a changed person, a young man with new hope, purpose and zest for life.

I sat next to Mom and Dad in a comfortable, white, stuffed armchair. We exchanged a few inanities about my life on the mobile fund-raising team, and our conversation bumped along, awkward and tense. More than every before, I sensed the yawning chasm which separated me from my family and everything they stood for. I felt as if I were speaking to Mom and Dad from inside a Plexiglass cube. And when I fell silent the sense of separation intensified and changed into total detachment.

Then, only the shell of my body would stare out from the armchair while my mind wandered back to the world of Sun Myung Moon and my True Brothers and Sisters.

My junior-high-school brother and sister were destroying a monstrous cardboard box, trying to get at the contents. Eric pulled out wads of crumpled newspaper until his chair was buried in them and Ingrid sat on the rug giggling. Finally he pulled out a small, long, flat package at the bottom of the box. "Wow. A piece of giant Super Stick Gum and a giant comb!" Eric ran the two-foot neon green comb through his hair and everyone laughed.

I felt sad that I was no longer as close to my blood brothers and one sister as I once had been. We used to get along so well. Now within them smoldered a sense of shame that their oldest brother had joined the strange and controversial following of Sun Myung Moon. This hurt because I wanted their respect and support.

The most disconcerting aspect of this estrangement was the chasm that gaped between me and my mother and father. At one point I caught Mom staring at me. I guessed she felt the distance too. Somehow, in the last two years we had lost all basis for communication. I used to love Mom as I loved dear life; we were close and I could talk to her about anything. Now, not even the smallest patch of common ground existed between us. I no longer respected Mom's and Dad's values, beliefs or life-style. And they didn't seem to think too highly of mine. Why did it have to be this way? I longed for the day when my entire family would believe in and follow the True Parents, when we could joke around and talk freely and easily like we used to. Then I could feel close to Mom and Dad and feel the old warmth between us.

But I didn't appreciate their laying the blame for all this psychological and emotional division on the Unification Church! It was their fault for not understanding the Divine Principle (the New Truth), and for not recognizing Reverend Moon as a great man, the new Messiah, the last Messiah.

After two years I'd come to accept the reality of that seemingly impenetrable wall. I finally realized that I couldn't relax and feel at home with my physical family because it wasn't home anymore. These people were not my true parents, not my true family, not truly my people. And I no longer cared what my parents thought of me. I despised their sick, evil-infested wasteland of a planet. (Righteous contempt!) I'd pretty much given up hope that Dad and Mom would ever see the light. They would never understand my world of good and evil spirits or realize that through the Unification Church God was establishing the Kingdom of heaven on earth.

At five o'clock the next day the whole family drove down to the Youngs's house for coffee. The Youngs were friends of my parents. I sauntered into the den and whooped when I saw good old Jim Britt leaning against the bureau with his hands in his pockets, as always. I grabbed his hand and we shook.

"Hey, Jim. Wow! What are you doing here?" Jim and I were lifelong buddies; we had grown up together on Bastian Road. But he looked unusually glum as he mumbled a greeting. Then his gaze dropped to stare at the Persian rug.

I suddenly noticed a hulking, young guy with wavy blond hair and a pro-boxer's jaw standing behind Jim. I introduced myself with a firm handshake and a 100-watt smile.

"Vick Minichello," he said. His face remained as closed up and hard as an oyster's. Then I heard Mom saying something. "Steve, I'd like you to meet Sharon Tyler."

I turned. A small crowd had gathered and a short, pudgy-faced girl with long black hair stood directly below me. She studied my face with a flicker of amusement in her eyes. Was I supposed to know her? No one said anything. Everyone's eyes were trained on me as if they were waiting for me to yell, "Go!" so they could sprint away for a game of hide-and-go-seek. The cheerful grin drained off my face.

Mom took my right hand in both of her hands and gently pulled me around to face her. Our eyes met. She had those tremulous lips and that funny shimmer in her eyes, the kind she always had when she was going to ask for a big favor.

"Steve—Sharon was a member of the Unification Church in the New England area for a year and a half. These people are here to help you. We're all here . . ." Her voice faded out and tears welled up in the corners of her eyes. She blinked and a thin stream trickled down one cheek. "We're here to help you. We love you and want you back . . . I want you back home."

I ignored my mother and threw an arcing glance around the room. Strong arms and bodies blocked the way to the sliding door on my right—my father, Hubert and Bruce. A monstrous bookcase covered the entire wall on my left. In front of me, at the far end of the den, a small grey couch stood beneath two windows. But they were latched shut and shielded by venetian blinds. Everything knotted up inside my chest and began to ache with resentment and a sickening helplessness. Surrounded. This was Satan's work—a deprogramming!

"Please listen to them, Steve," said Mom. "That's all we want you to do. Will you sit down and listen to what they have to say?" Fear and dark, desperate thoughts surrounded me. It seemed that hours of staring at each other's gaunt faces passed before I decided that there was no use in trying to fight my way out.

"OK, OK. I'll listen. But it's not going to do any good. You're not going to change my mind about anything." My voice sounded muffled and far away as if a ventriloquist spoke through me.

I eased myself down on to the couch, warily, half fearing that it would spring a stranglehold on me. Only one thing remained clear in my confusion, Satan was all around. He masterminded the entire operation, possessed the deprogrammers, spoke through them. I felt drugged and numbed by shock. Mom and Dad had betrayed me, surrendered to the evil spiritual powers. Now Satan was working through them more than ever before.

The restoration of the world through the Lord of the Second Advent would mean the end to Satan's dominion over the earth. Though I was only one person, as a follower of the new Messiah I posed an incredible threat to Satan. Even if he had to pick us off one by one he was determined to destroy us.

A coffee table stood between my sofa and the wooden chairs where Vick and Sharon were sitting. My parents, brothers and Jim sat behind the two deprogrammers in kitchen chairs. A panorama of satanic faces. Sharon wore black pants and a black sweater with a small cross and chain around her neck. *Black like Satan,* I thought. I'd learned that the eyes of fallen-world people look shadow-ringed and sunken because they're spiritually dead. And sure enough, the death look of Satan's world smoldered in their eyes. I could almost see the evil spirits, the agents of the Evil One, slithering, floating and slinking in the warm air of the room.

I'd heard gruesome stories about how kidnapped members had been tied up in chairs and beaten. Probably any minute now some six-feet-four-inch linebacker-ape would push back the sliding door and clomp in with an armful of rope.

Sharon must have noticed the glint of terror in my eyes. She slid her chair closer to the coffee table and said, "Steve, we're here because your parents want you to hear the other side of the story, the one insiders never hear about." She assured me that I didn't have to be afraid. If I really had the truth then there was absolutely no reason to be afraid.

The crowded den was like an operating room with doctors and nurses slipping quietly in and out. Two seconds after Bruce went out, Dad squeezed in. He was followed by a short young man with solid black-frame glasses and curly black hair. After flooring a bulging black leather briefcase he walked straight up to me, flashed a mellow smile and extended his hand.

"Hi, I'm Phil Epstein." I wanted to ignore him, but he seemed so sincere. Slowly, I uncrossed my arms, shook his hand and gave him a curt nod, then returned to the defiant crossed-arm position. Phil sat down on the other half of the couch and took a large, black Bible out of his briefcase and began to leaf through it. He felt we should go over some of the numerous discrepancies and distortions in the *Divine Principle's* interpretation of the Bible.

"There are no discrepancies or distortions in the *Divine Principle.* You're just interpreting the Bible incorrectly." I said this as coolly and as matter-of-factly as I could. But I felt like shouting it. Phil responded by saying that "Mr. Moon, like many false religious leaders, reads his own interpretation into Bible passages in order to support his own pet cosmic-spiritual ideology. He takes from the Bible whatever supports his divine revelation and ignores or rejects as non-applicable everything that contradicts it."

In spite of the circumstances, Phil seemed like an easy-going, mellow guy. I liked him almost immediately. His warm, relaxed and empathic way was disarming. Sharon and Vick were more intense. Phil spoke amicably, as if he were a close buddy and fellow student who was tutoring me in a subject I was bungling.

Phil shifted on the sofa. "For example, based on Luke 1:56, which mentions that Mary spent three months at the home of Zacharias and Elizabeth, the parents of John the Baptist, the great decoder Moon figures out that Jesus is the bastard son of Zacharias and Mary." I flinched, surprised that they knew about this little known inner teaching.

Phil, Vick and Sharon continued citing discrepancies in the *Divine Principle*'s interpretation of the Bible. But their arguments and interrogations ricocheted off my mind like buckshot spraying tank armor. Why?

Well, in the first place, there was no point in listening to them or to any fallen person for that matter—I had the whole truth, the complete, flawless and absolute truth. And secondly, the deprogrammers were the agents of Satan and everything they said came from Satan. Sharon sounded like a screeching old Wicked Witch of the West. If I closed my eyes for a few seconds, I sensed the evil spirits hovering over her head, whispering lies and accusations to her mind; weapons with which to sever my allegiance to the one Satan feared most— Sun Myung Moon.

Nothing they said sank in, nothing made an impression, absolutely nothing. My armor seemed virtually impenetrable and I was confident I could hold out forever. After two hours I noticed that they still hadn't done anything rash like tying me up in a chair and slapping me with the backs of their hands.

That's when I regained my usual confidence and decided to convert everyone in the room to the side of the True Parents. The fear dissipated like morning fog, and for the rest of the night I felt like a monarch on his throne. Below my couch-pedestal rallied a band of peasants. I was absolutely confident that I could convert the entire thickheaded, sordid gang, not only my family and the deprogrammers, but also the family friends who'd dropped in to see me during the past two hours— mathematicians, doctors, a chemist and an architect.

Into the wee hours we haggled and debated. Phil, Vick or Sharon would confront me with a supposed contradiction in our ideology and I would try to straighten them out by lecturing from the *Divine Principle*.

First, Phil discussed the *Divine Principle's* chapter on the fall of man. He argued that one couldn't conclude, based on the evidence in Genesis, that "eating the fruit" referred to an illicit sexual relationship with Eve and Lucifer and then between Eve and Adam. I began my counterattack by saying that Adam and Eve covered their lower parts because it was a human trait to hide evidence of criminal activity or wrongdoing.

Then Sharon attempted to show how the *Divine Principle's* teaching about Jesus' failure to complete His mission was false. She quoted from a passage in John 17: "When Jesus had spoken these words, he lifted up his eyes to heaven and said, 'Father, the hour has come; glorify thy Son that the Son may glorify thee, . . . I glorified thee on earth, having accomplished the work which thou gavest me to do' " (vv. 1,4). I responded by saying that John was putting words in Jesus' mouth in order to make them consistent with the theology he was developing for the early church.

Around and around we went, hour after hour, exchanging a so-called "Divine Principle" contradiction or biblical distortion for a section I had practically memorized from the D.P. or for an argument the Church had developed to counter criticisms.

Around three o'clock in the morning Sharon threw up her arms and cried, "My God, you think you have an answer for everything! In a way you do, only they're not answers; they're slick rationalizations, robot responses that you spout off without thinking." Sharon said I was parroting the Moon doctrine in almost the exact same way she had rattled it off during her deprogramming, the same words and word order.

"But this is what I really *believe!*" I yelled back. She replied that my belief wasn't based on personal investigation of the *Divine Principle* and the Bible. Most Moonies, she claimed, don't have any intelligent understanding of the Bible upon which the *Divine Principle* is almost entirely based, nor have they ever read the whole D.P. book. (She was definitely right on those points.)

"You believe all that nonsense because it's been drummed into your head in the course of a score of workshops."

Phil sat on the lip of the sofa facing me. He was leaning forward with his arms on his knees, shaking his head slowly.

"Wow, Steve, I forgot how trapped I was, trapped in that same controlled state of mind and web of lies and rationalizations you're trapped in now." He explained how rationalization is a key element in maintaining the delusion of which Unification Church members are victims, the delusion that they're helping the Messiah to build the perfect world of the last days. Rationalizing helps to produce a consistency in the way one views the ideology and experiences life in the group. In this way it works as a survival mechanism which protects members from the anguish of constant doubt. When Phil was in the group, if any inconsistencies in the doctrine or practices confronted him, such as the way they lied about where the money was going when they fund-raised, he said he would rationalize it away: "Oh, we're taking money from Satan and giving it back to God, so it's OK."

The room fell silent for a moment. It was getting late and most everyone had left except the deprogrammers, my parents and Bruce. Vick leaned over and picked up a leftover soup cracker from the table. The cracker made a loud crunch when he sank his teeth into it. Then he leaned back in his chair and looked me up and down like a stern cop who'd caught me doing 95.

"Hell, you're not capable of any original or creative thought anymore," his heavy Philadelphia accent spiced every word. "Your parents were telling me how you used to be a bright, energetic little guy, a pretty good student too, and you used to write poetry and short stories and things. All I see now is a carbon copy of every Moonie I've ever met in the two years since my brother joined Moon's cult."

That night Dad slept on the floor next to the couch. The ceiling fixture in the hall cast streams of light through the cracks in the door. I could hear a chair creaking in the hallway. One of my father's mathematician colleagues was doing all-night guard duty outside the door. I lay stretched out on the couch, staring up into the darkness. For 20 minutes I murmured a desperate prayer: "Oh heavenly Father! Help me to survive this deprogramming, help me to get back to the Family, back to the True Parents." I closed my prayer in "the name of the True Parents," rolled on my side and closed my eyes.

Chapter Two

Escape?

*"Whatever crushes individuality is
despotism by whatever name it
may be called,"
John Stuart Mill.*

Dishes streaked with spaghetti sauce covered the table. The afternoon winter sun trickled through the blinds and shed a pale light on Mom's hands as she cleared away the cups and silverware. This was the second day of my "captivity." Vick sat with his back to the bookcase; a portable tape recorder lay in front of him on the end of the table. He was going to run a few tapes about other groups: Hare Krishna, the Children of God, Brother Julius, Scientology, the Forever Family (or Church of Bible Understanding) and several others.

"All these cults operate similarly," said Vick. "They all employ deception to recruit members and they all use fear, guilt and other forms of psychological manipulation to keep their members in. And Sun Myung Moon is just one of the many cult leaders, although his cult is one of the largest and most notorious."

We listened to the tapes for a couple hours. I laughed at how bizarre these groups were. Brother Julius Christ believes he's the reincarnation of Jesus Christ. David (Moses) Berg, leader of the Children of God and prophet of the end-times, loves to discuss sex in some of his "Mo-letters" to the members. Hare Krishna believes that men's brains are larger than women's brains; and the menfolk wear ponytails so that at the moment of death Lord Krishna can pull them up to heaven. The tapes made no impression other than their ridiculousness. *Impos-*

ters! I laughed to myself. *Just counterfeits of the Unification Church.*

But nothing that happened after that seemed very funny. As we careened into the second day of the deprogramming it became clear that I wasn't about to convert *anyone* to the Unification Church. My only hope was to prove that I would never break, that my belief in the *Divine Principle* and my loyalty to Sun Myung Moon were unshakable. Eventually they'd have to let me go. Still, the original fear of Satan and the sense of doom seeped back into my heart and began eating at my faith.

Deprogramming was certainly not the horror story the Family made it out to be. Sometimes we just talked. Or Sharon and Phil would describe their experiences in the Unification Church and explain what aspects of the group had caused them to decide to leave it. Meanwhile, Mom scurried around constantly, preparing meals, snacks and drinks, asking me if I wanted anything. A love so intense shone in my parents' eyes that I felt ashamed at times.

The Family always portrayed deprogramming as part of a hate campaign bent on destroying the Unification Church. That's why I was taken aback when everyone around me, especially the deprogrammers, expressed so much love and concern for me. The deprogrammers were so obviously sincere. I'd always assumed that they deprogrammed simply for the money, but I soon realized that it was a hellish way to earn a buck, and they ran a high risk of being sued or jailed.

Through the blinds I saw the late morning sun of the third day reflecting off the snow in the yard. I let the water run in the bathroom sink so no one could hear me fumbling with the window. The best time to break out would be just after dark. But I wanted to be sure the window would open before I made the attempt. My heart did a wild African drumbeat and the palms of my hands were moist as I raised the blinds. The latches on the inside screen clicked open easily enough. I squeezed my hand behind the screen to unfasten the window latch. Then I gave the window frame a firm push, expecting it to swing outward on its rusty hinges. The top and middle of the window gave way, but the bottom wouldn't budge. And I couldn't see what was holding it in place. I didn't shove the window too hard for fear it would make too much noise. By this time my hands were shaking. After a little more prying and pushing I refastened the latch and put the screen back in place. *Tonight. Tonight the bottom would give way. It had to.*

They had torn Father to pieces last night. Sharon had horrified everyone with accounts of how several ex-Moonies wound up in psychiatric wards. They'd either been haunted by fear and guilt at having deserted the Messiah, or completely spent by the trauma of trying to assimilate into the outside world, or both.

Sharon related the story of the early days of the Korean Church—couples had sometimes left their babies in garbage cans to die. I'd heard about these tragedies before from the higher-ups and understood that there'd been barely enough food for the *parents* to keep from starving to death. But why then, asked Vick, had Sun Myung Moon continued to receive the choicest foods?

"And what about all the heavenly deception, Steve?" Sharon had asked. "I know kids who were saying the money went to drug rehab centers, Christian youth centers or prison reform. Do you think the public would donate millions of dollars every year if they knew where the money really went?" I shifted uncomfortably in my seat and tried to hide a deep, dry swallow.

Later on, smack in the middle of everything, Vick laughed out loud at something he'd been reading in "Master Speaks," a collection of speeches given by Father at special Family gatherings. "Hey get this. I just found a real prizewinner. Straight from the ass's mouth, 'Out of all the saints sent by God, I think I am the most successful one . . . Don't you think so?' "[1]

Everyone (except me) threw their heads back and roared. But it was true that he'd said that once. And he was always bragging about his endurance under the communist imprisonment during the Korean War and about how God loved him more than anyone.

Around 1:00 A.M. Vick had said, "Who do you think Sun Myung Moon is *now*, Steve?" When I played the clam he stopped rocking in his chair and let the front legs thud back onto the floor. "We're going to stay here for four days or four months, as long as you want. It's up to you. If that's what it will take, we're all willing to make that sacrifice."

I thought, *Wow, that's a long time!* And the very idea of trying to hold out for four months made me shiver. But on the outside I was still defiant. I sat up straight and began speaking strongly about freedom of religion, the first amendment, and about the Unification Church being a victim of cruel religious persecution.

Phil propped himself on his elbows. "You Moonies are always screaming about freedom of religion and religious persecution, but you refuse to deal with the issue of mind manipulation and mental coercion used to induct members and keep them in the group." Phil explained how isolation and nonstop indoctrination work powerfully on a young recruit. And this manipulation and coercion quash the ability to think and choose freely. Before there can be freedom of religion—free choices in terms of religion—there must first be freedom of thought.

Then Phil went on to describe the role of deception in the cult induction process. "In the first place," said Phil, "a newcomer isn't told about Moon's more bizarre beliefs and rituals until *after* he joins. And he's never informed as to what his responsibilities as a member are; so the guy has no idea how much he will be forced to give up if he joins."

I wedged myself back into the couch and crossed my arms. "You people accuse the Unification Church of brainwashing. But what you're doing—*deprogramming*—is actually brainwashing."

But then Phil pointed out that there was a very important difference between deprogramming and brainwashing; nor was deprogramming simply brainwashing in reverse. "Brainwashing," said Epstein, "funnels a person into a rigid and controlled state of mind and absolutely dictates group belief. Deprogramming doesn't 'brainwash' a person into *another* controlled state of mind, nor does it dictate what a person should believe."

Suddenly Epstein jerked up from his crouch like a man startled out of sleep. "Rather, deprogramming *frees* a person from the cultic state of mind, and enables him to think for himself again and decide for himself what he's going to believe."

I sat perched on the edge of the couch, my fingernails digging into the cushions. All these discussions about mind control, thought reform and how I was brainwashed simply infuriated me! Made me so angry! I just didn't think there was anything wrong with my behavior or the way I thought. And I couldn't counter all their psychology so I tried to drag the argument into a different ball field.

"But this is kidnapping! You're kidnapping me and that's not right!"

"Kidnapping?" said Sharon. "This isn't kidnapping; it's a rescue mission. My father had me deprogrammed last year and I'll be grateful to him for the rest of my life! It's like there was barbed wire around my mind." She explained how in a concentration camp a person sees the barbed wire, knows he's imprisoned and can thus try to escape. but in a cult the barbed wire is the ironhanded control the group exercises over your mind; you don't even know it's there, so you can't break free. You don't realize you're a prisoner. "My Dad didn't kidnap me. He rescued me!"

Yet I could only pity Sharon and her family. Someday in the course of eternity they would discover what they had done to their daughter, and they would pull their hair out by the roots in mortification for having rejected the Messiah. I stared at her without meaning to stare, hating her. Here was something worse than a non-member—a defector from the True Family of God.

Peter leaned over and fished a bulging folder of loose papers out of his briefcase. He wanted to define exactly what he meant by the term *cult.* And he felt that Jean Merritt, a psychiatric social worker who has worked with hundreds of ex-cult members, gave a good definition of this term in her statements on cults. He quoted her: "We define Rev. Moon's Unification Church, Hare Krishna, Children of God and other such groups as religious cults. We do not consider them a religion because the loyalty of their members is not to a formalized doctrine, but solely to the dictums of a leader, one person. Because of this, rules, regulations and beliefs vary with the whim of the leader. Power and control are in his hands and no one else's. The closest analogy is that of a dictatorship or of a totalitarian state."[2]

After another two hours of this verbal warfare I had finally gone to bed, exhausted and not nearly as clear-headed and confident as 24 hours before.

My whole body had shuddered that third morning when my eyes opened to the same guarded room, the same sofa, and to my father snoring gently on the floor again. Then a feeling of desperation had burst in my stomach and started gnawing at my insides. It must have been around 7:00 A.M. Burying my head in the pillows of the couch I'd tried to visualize Father. But all I could muster was the image of a cold, heartless Oriental man in a black suit. Even after an hour of silently chanting and praying I couldn't feel a gram of love for this man who I believed was my spiritual father and Lord.

I must have lain there for hours, my faced mashed into the sofa cushions. No matter how hard I prayed and chanted I couldn't regain a connection with the True Parents. And after the decade of the past two days even the Brothers and Sisters seemed as strange and far away as the Messiah and his wife. Light years away. I began thinking, "Is there really a Sun Myung Moon? a Sun Myung Moon who represents the Second Advent of Christ?" Suddenly the last two years of my life seemed like an eerie dream, an endless dream of wandering in the bowels of a shadowy, howling wasteland. And on and off, like flashes of lightning, I kept slipping down into the same haunting thoughts—that the Unification Church was some bizarre, distasteful fantasy-world which existed only in my mind.

I began thinking how nice it would be to take a vacation from the gruelling 15-hour-day fund-raising grind and the too-short four hours of sleep per night. Then it struck me: *Hey, I could just go along with them and fake it. Tell them I've seen the light.* Then I could relax for a few weeks and enjoy myself, sit around and read novels, go skiing and to the movies. Ahhh! Some peace and some time to myself. I was weary, so weary. I'd given everything to these last two years and it seemed I'd received almost nothing in return. Rest. To rest just for a short while. Then of course after a few weeks I'd go back.

That's when I caught myself. Satan! Satan's trying to tempt me, trying to drag me away from the Family. Heavenly Father, give me strength. Help me to fight it. I'm beginning to go! What my pride and self-confidence had told me would never happen was happening! My faith, my very spirit had reached the breaking point. It was time to get out of there, fast. That's when I tested the bathroom window.

By five o'clock of that third day the crowd had thinned out again leaving only Phil, Sharon and my parents. Since we'd started the day five-and-a-half hours ago I hadn't fired back more than a few sentences. My new strategy was to refuse to respond to any more of their questions and accusations. The long days of defending my position had left me tired and psychologically worn out. My speech was beginning to slur. My shoulders slumped as if I'd aged 50 years in three days. My spine felt like a spaghetti noodle. Most disconcerting of all, my True Parents and Brothers and Sisters still seemed very far away, aeons, galaxies, dream-worlds away. *That's exactly what Satan wants,* I thought, *he wants to wear me down with all this negative give and take.* Instead of listening to Dad I was silently chanting and praying my brains out, begging God to reenergize me with my former conviction. I even tried to visualize Father sitting on the sofa talking calmly and giving me moral support.

"You know, Steve," said Dad, "you may think you've grown and spiritually advanced a great deal in these past two years. But you've actually become very narrowed, almost stale." He asked me if I remembered how I used to kid Eric and Ingrid, constantly thinking of new names to call them, like "Clanky Doo-Van-Doo" and "Ingy Butt-Too-Big." I grunted an acknowledgment. Dad went on to remind me how I used to horse around during dinner cleanup, imitating Humphrey Bogart, foreign accents and singing camp and pop songs at the top of my lungs.

My father said all those things were gone now—the richness of language, the idiosyncracies, all those characteristics that defined me as a unique human being. Now I spoke with a smaller, carefully constricted vocabulary with many clichés and stereotyped ideas. My style of language and of relating had become so constricted because I'd been molded to conform to Moon's model of the "heavenly child." It was as if someone had taken a knife and chisel to my mind and whittled me down to the bare core of the person I had once been.

"I wish to heck you'd cut it out with all that mind control garbage." This was my first verbal response in over two hours and I drawled it out in a bored voice. Suddenly Mom's hand smacked down on the flat, wooden arm of her chair. I returned a look of arrogant nonchalance.

"Look at you!" yelled my mother. "This whole time you've been nothing but a benign, placid lump. You never really get angry, your eyes never dilate. And you speak without any emotion, while all of us here have been pouring out our hearts and minds, everything, to try to get through to you."

Dad had crossed his arms on his chest and was frowning. "Mom's right, Steve. Sure, your intellect is working in that you can throw back arguments, as mindless and dogmatic as they are. But there is no heart, no emotion behind your arguments."

Mom let go a wail, "I just can't stand it anymore! For the last three days you've been sitting there with the same benign smirk on your face, unscathed by whatever we say, and talking down to us as if we were a bunch of stupid, pitiful children."

"And that brings up another subject," said Sharon. "Who are your true parents?" I groaned inwardly and felt like ripping her head off for bringing that up. There was a stretch of silence that lasted about three geologic ages. Sharon slid to the edge of her chair. "Why can't you answer your parents?"

Mom rose from her chair and pushed the coffee table that stood between us until it made a sound thud against the bookcase. Then she straightened herself to face me. A silvery thread of tears edged down her cheek. Dad stood behind Mom with that same hurt look in his eyes. Mom's hands were wringing an imaginary dish towel. "Steve, answer us!"

Sharon had crossed the room and stood at my left, leaning just a couple feet from my face. "Steve, who are your true parents, your real true parents?" I threw her a stare of daggers. "These people standing here loved you with everything in their hearts—for 20 years. Please tell us who your true parents are. Is it going to be your own mother and father or that fat Korean who doesn't even know you exist?"

My eyes were boring holes in the wall behind them. Anger, bitterness and a touch of shame churned like grimy sludge in a washing machine. On the one hand was my cold, unquestioning loyalty to Sun Myung Moon and the True Family, a ruthless and powerful allegiance. On the other hand I felt the shame beating on the walls of that heartless and blind devotion. Mom and Dad had given me so much love during my 18 years at home, and so much encouragement. But I couldn't feel a trace of love for them anymore. Now I despised them because they were trying to take me away from God.

"Please answer them, Steve. Who are your true parents?" By this time Mom and Dad were gawking in disbelief as if their son had just pumped a few slugs into their stomachs. Several moments of silence passed before my mother screamed, "Look what they've done to my son! He's not a human being *at all*. He's nothing but a heartless zombie." She dragged herself to a chair and buried her face in her hands. A wretched sob shook her body as she began crying. Then Dad strode to her side to caress her shoulders.

I tried to ignore this display of emotion by staring at the bookcase. But Dad caught my eye for a second. He gave me a How-could-you-do-this-to-your-mother? kind of look. I turned away to stare at the paintings on the opposite wall. I felt the same, the old nostalgia of a love that once flowed so warm and solid between us beating on the iron casing of my mind. But my anger and my devotion to the other "Parents" would not let it in.

By 5:30 everyone was ready for a break. I still refused to respond and they were tired of pleading and lecturing to a human wall. Everybody left the room except Bruce and Phil.

It's now or never, I thought. I turned to Phil, "I'm going to take a shower if you don't mind." He nodded. Bruce got up and followed me to the bathroom and posted himself outside the door.

My hands were shaking slightly as I closed the door. I didn't have much time. I had to work fast. Immediately I turned on the shower so my brother wouldn't hear anything. "Help me get out of here, heavenly Father," I prayed. Soon the screen was leaning against the wall. I unfastened the latch, placed my right hand on the base of the window frame and applied a strong, steady pressure.

Above the sound of the streaming shower a voice of fear echoed in my head. *You must get away. You must get away.*

"Come on, come on!" I muttered under my breath. I pushed hard, not daring to pound. I strained till I could feel the blood bulging in my eyes and the beads of sweat popping through my forehead. But the bottom of the window would not budge.

There was only one thing left to do. I took several steps backwards till my back touched the door. Aiming my shoulder I hurled myself across the room into the window. The sound of my body hitting the glass and metal came first, then the screech of metal scraping metal as the window gave a little.

Like a bad dream of plummeting down into a canyon I saw myself bouncing off the window into the sink behind me. The very bottom inch of the window had refused to yield. The bathroom door smashed against the wall. Bruce stood in the doorway, his face a terrified gargoyle. He bellowed, "He's trying to get away! Steve's trying to get away!"

I made one last desperate lunge at the window. Again it screeched and threw me back into the sink. Within a second Bruce had come up from behind and locked his arms around my shoulders. The house began stomping and yelling as if a great fire had broken out. Mom sounded as if she was being stabbed to death, "Don't let him get away! Oh don't let him get away."

Like a sweating, English rugby team the men in the house dragged their writhing human football out of the bathroom. In the tangle of earnest faces I could recognize only Dad's face close to mine. Iron hands gripped my arms and shoulders as I tried to fight back.

A sickening sense of defeat came like vomit into my chest and throat. I was fighting for my spiritual life. My parents were fighting to get their son back. Yet I saw myself as the victim of an evil plot. The members of my own family were accomplices in a diabolical plan to spiritually murder me.

For three days they had pleaded and argued and cried in an effort to draw me back to their world. They were trying desperately to build a bridge to cross the gaping chasm that had come between us. I knew that they loved me, that they were doing everything only because they loved me. But as I lay sprawled against the end of the couch, breathing hard, my only thought was: *Get out of here before you are lost forever.*

Chapter Three

Encounter

"There is not a heart but has its moments of longing, yearning for something better, nobler, holier than it knows now,"
Henry Ward Beecher.

Chilled wind and rain brushed my face as I stepped off the plane in Oakland, California. It didn't seem fair that it had to rain my first day in. I'd been looking forward to going to school in sun-filled Berkeley for over six months, and looking forward to going to college for over four years.

Classes didn't start until the first of October, but I came out ten days early to find a place to live. The housing division had fouled things up—I hadn't been assigned to a dorm room and now every space was filled.

I boarded a bus and we began climbing and coasting through the dripping hills of Oakland towards the University of California at Berkeley. As I stared out the window at swaying eucalyptus trees and white stucco Spanish-style houses I reminisced on how Berkeley had been in 1966-67 when we had been here with Dad, on sabbatical leave from Stanford. I never forgot the gay, unrestrained, turbulent spirit of Berkeley—the anti-war rallies, the irate student speakers, the street artists and musicians, the flowers, peace signs and long hair. I was only 12 at the time, but no one had to tell me that here was a community with hope and determination to revolutionize, to find new and more meaningful ways of perceiving and living.

As we drove toward the university I struck up a conversa-

tion with a young woman next to me. As if the drizzling rain
didn't accentuate my homeless state enough, she described the
tough housing situation around the Berkeley campus. "Yeah,
you'll probably have to live way off campus, buy a car and
commute," she said. I gulped and wondered what I was doing
here and what exactly had happened to my sunny California.

Once in Berkeley I checked my stuff into a campus hotel and
went down to the housing office. I talked to a housing official
and the dorm situation still looked bleak. After flipping
through listings of off-campus housing for a couple hours I
decided to take a break and explore the campus.

> September, 1973
> Dear Mom and Dad, Bruce, Hubert, Ingrid and Eric,
>   Well hello from Berkeley! We're having the most
> fantastic weather here. How's it in Rochester? Sproul
> Plaza is the funniest place in the afternoon. Little
> hick-country bands are playing under the trees, us-
> ing some of the craziest instruments (e.g. kazoos
> made of beer cans, . . .). Then there's this guy who
> stands on the fountain and screams out, "The flying
> saucers are coming man! Watch out, here they come!"

I wandered, or rather stumbled onto Sproul Plaza. The view
enchanted me as would a clearing in a great forest filled with
dancing, singing, merry elves. Near the student union, in the
full warmth of the afternoon sun, a small gathering danced and
clapped to the beat of Congo drums. Pairs of students passed
out pamphlets and brochures to the river of people sweeping
over the plaza. On the plaza steps and on the fountain young
people sat around munching sandwiches and fruit. A long line
of card tables stretched along the thoroughfare where repre-
sentatives of everything from the Young Socialists to the local
yogi ashram distributed literature and information.

Eventually, the guy preaching from the fountain lost his
audience to a purple-cloaked, top-hatted fire breather. For a
while I forgot about my housing problem. I was fascinated,
enchanted and somewhat bewildered by this cultural, political
and spiritual supermarket. It was true. I was in Berkeley, a
teeming mecca of sorts, an education center which would ex-

pose me to a wide array of life-styles, nationalities and points of view. And I had four years to explore this mecca and tap its resources.

My third day in town the housing office guaranteed me an overflow room (in this case, a converted lounge) in a dorm on High Street. What a relief! I had a place to live. I went out to eat that night in a Mexican restaurant on Telegraph Avenue, the main drag through Berkeley. I ate tamales and watched the street artists pack up their wares for the day—leather bags and belts, wood sculptures and drawings.

After I grew tired of looking out the window into the scurrying dusk of Telegraph Avenue, I began staring into my coffee. I couldn't believe I was really in Berkeley. I kept imagining that if I looked up from my warm brew I'd find myself back in Amsterdam (where I'd gone to high school for a year) or home in Rochester. I had looked forward to coming out to the West Coast for such a long time and now I was here. At least a thousand times I must have hummed the words to the 1972 top tune, "It never rains in Southern California" and thought with warm yearning of that western land of sunshine.

Coming to Berkeley was the conscious beginning of a new life—out of the house, out of the high-school scene, off to the opposite side of the North American continent. This was definitely a new beginning.

Why then were my feelings so surprisingly mixed? I felt excitement. Yet I also felt uneasiness and disappointment. On one hand UC Berkeley impressed me in terms of what it had to offer: a fine education, sunshine, and a vibrant, youthful and active community—a goldmine of options and opportunity. Already, I was looking forward to doing some volunteer work in the Bay Area as I had at the Monroe County Youth Counseling Center in Rochester. I had also worked with a 19-year-old man, crippled with cerebral palsy, during my senior year in Holland. I had enjoyed these experiences and wanted to try more volunteer work to see if social work might be my bag.

I also looked forward to meeting good people and making good friends. In this sense especially, I found Berkeley intensely exciting. The community brought together people from many backgrounds, nationalities and life-styles. And in this cultural goldmine I could mingle with and learn from people who were active, articulate, inquisitive—people who were trying new things out, delving, developing, in order to live lives that would be as meaningful as possible.

I looked up and watched a guy wearing a red backpack come out of the Turkish coffeehouse across the street and stroll towards campus. This sparked memories of my hitchhiking-train tour of Europe that summer. The trip had been the fulfillment of so many dreams. I had looked forward to Berkeley in that same way, like another adventure. Only this wasn't a trip or a vacation; rather the shoving off of a new life. And the queasy uncertainty and uneasiness I felt dampened the excitement of arriving in my precious college town.

Why did my jump into college life seem more like a step out into thin air rather than a leap into another adventure? Why all the butterflies? I loved adventure, new experiences, new places and fresh viewpoints. I thrived on it. And this was certainly not my first time away from home. I'd already spent two summers by myself in Europe—one summer on a French farm, and one summer touring glorious Europe.

As I thought about it, there seemed to be two reasons for this uneasiness. For one thing, in spite of Berkeley's great assets, I was a little disappointed. Arriving in Berkeley turned out to be an anticlimactic experience. During four years of high school I'd looked forward to college. I had molded it into a dreamworld, built it up to be more than it was, and then arrived in Berkeley expecting more than Berkeley could give.

Aside from the university itself, I had expected a different kind of *Berkeley*. The Berkeley of 1967 had vanished—no more gay, hopeful spirit of the sixties. Political activism had been replaced by a certain apathy, a cynicism. Even the sidewalks and streets seemed more littered than they had been. The Berkeley that had lived in my mind all those years was a phantom. I realized this and felt disappointment.

The second reason for my disquiet was more serious and it surprised even me. I had always viewed myself as resourceful and independent. My wilderness canoe and camping trips and two European adventures had taught me a great deal about surviving in the world. Yet, as I sat alone in the restaurant—18 years old, fidgeting with my coffee—I suddenly felt so green, so new to the world, clumsy and not knowing what to expect.

I was anxious to get settled in a permanent living situation, to firmly plant two feet in California soil. The long-awaited dream was no longer a dream. It was called UC Berkeley. I was in it and it was my new life. Rationalizing, I hoped I wasn't the only college freshman living out these feelings.

One Monday afternoon, my fifth day in Berkeley, I was traversing Sproul Plaza when I noticed that an unusually large number of card tables had mushroomed along the thorough-fare. This was probably because classes were only a week away and students were flooding back into town. Pamphlets and books covered the tabletops. Colorful banners and posters proclaimed great events and causes—the Hillel Society, a Buddhist group, the Revolutionary Communist Youth Brigade, a university Christian fellowship, a voter registration table (looking very much out of place), and an organization brandishing a large poster which read "Ideal City Project."

The Ideal City poster intrigued me. I figured it represented some kind of community project. Since I was interested in anything that was working concretely to solve social problems I stepped out of the mainstream of passersby to investigate. A group of backpacked hitchhikers and young people were clustered around the table jabbering animatedly. I kept my distance, wanting to examine the poster before they hit me with a sales pitch. Photographs attached to the poster depicted a farming community set in lush, green rolling hills.

Suddenly a woman with short brown bangs, shiny eyes and a dimply smile skipped through the crowd and pushed a flyer into my hands. "Hi," she said. "My name's Arlane." And before I knew it I'd followed the friendly leafleter to the table and gotten myself invited to a free dinner and evening program at their house.

Arlane introduced me to her friends—Blossom, Sandra, Daniel and Warren. They all greeted me with warm flashing eyes and hearty handshakes. These people were different from everyone else I'd met in Berkeley so far. They seemed like such nice people. And they seemed so interested in me and in what I had to say. They listened to every word as if I might reveal the location of a lost gold city of the Incas. Arlane's big puppy-dog eyes gazed into mine without ever wavering. These folks radiated a certain peace and good will as if a halo of tranquility enveloped them and completely separated them from the cares and worries of everyday life.

The only thing that seemed strange was the conservative dress of the men. Their short hair, neat, light-colored shirts and narrow slacks looked out of place in Berkeley, California. Considering their exceptional friendliness, however, this didn't bother me much.

When I asked them what their work was about, Blossom spoke up. Apparently she supervised the table. "We work out of a couple of nice houses where we all live together [one was on Dana Street and the other on Regent Street]. We sponsor various community-oriented programs, like workshops for students and businessmen. And we run several businesses where people can be placed in jobs and gain excellent work experience. We're also planning to start a recycling program. One of our most exciting projects is our community farm, the Ideal City Project."

Blossom described the "Booneville farm" as a beautiful 640-acre chunk of land 160 miles north of Berkeley in Mendocino County. She spoke rather vaguely about the project. Basically, their goal was to establish an international model community.

Without much hesitation I accepted their invitation to dinner. I was intrigued. What kind of group is this? What kind of work are they doing? What makes them tick? From what they had told me I gathered I was attending a dinner and slide presentation sponsored by a community-oriented young people's cooperative. In any case, I believed I could learn something from this very warm, serene and friendly bunch of people.

We pulled up in front of a tidy, white wooden house with a rock garden and a porch. Over 20 cars were parked bumper to bumper up and down the street: convertibles, vans, Mustangs, Volkswagens, "Man, are these all your cars?!" asked a dinner-guest in the back seat. Arlane nodded.

The porch jostled with people trying to file inside. I climbed the steps and saw that most of the porch was carpeted with rows of shoes, sneakers and sandals. "Keeps the house clean," laughed Arlane as she plopped her Earth Shoes in one of the rows. I followed suit. Then she led me into a living room packed with young people. The air buzzed with talk and small groups of twos and threes stood or squatted on the huge expanse of yellow shag rug. For a second I imagined I'd stumbled upon a lively high school reunion. Everyone seemed very much at ease, and a soothing pleasant atmosphere filled the room.

At the far end of the room two aproned girls were thudding pots and bowls of zucchini, rice, fruit salad and Kool-aid on a large coffee table. A minute later I was squished in a circle of 40 people, assembled around the table holding our evening meal. A skinny young man with a 200-watt smile stood at one end of the table. With his hair cropped especially short he looked as if he'd just come out of basic training. He wore a yellow short-sleeved shirt and a thin green tie which had somehow survived the 1950s.

"Hi everyone! My name's Luke, and we welcome you to our New Education Family." He thanked us for coming and outlined the evening agenda: a delicious dinner, entertainment and then a lecture program. Luke gestured like an Italian—swinging his arms together into a strong clasp and then throwing them outwards again. And he projected the brilliant glow of a pulsating lighthouse, a bubbly, joyous spirit that was amusing and uplifting. I liked him immediately.

Then they passed out songbooks and a dark, frizzy-haired woman carrying a guitar padded up to Luke's side. Luke introduced her as Christine. Her nose, chin and mouth were sharp and beautiful. She looked like an alluring gypsy with her long, thick hair bundled back in a red and yellow bandana. Singing in a robust, clear voice, and slashing down hard on the guitar strings, she led us in "Down by the Riverside." Soon the entire room sang, clapped and swayed in time.

As we rocked through songs like "Save the Country" and "Blowing in the Wind" my gaze swept the myriad of cheery and luminous faces. It seemed that an interesting cross-section of society had gathered in the room that night. Besides the group members, who made up about half of the crowd, there were sunburned hitchhikers (probably in California for the first time), seasoned local "freaks," a smattering of younger looking student-types, a few black brothers, and even two uniformed men from the Oakland naval base. Everyone seemed to be as swept up as I was in a spirit of enthusiasm and good will.

I'd never heard the last song we sang—Luke mentioned that someone in the group had written it. "Gonna Build a Kingdom" had a vigorous and powerful beat and I found myself clapping and stomping my feet by the middle of the song. Arlane and I looked at each other, grinning and laughing.

> *Gonna build a Kingdom in this sad old land,*
> *Gonna build a Kingdom, it's at hand,*
> *Gonna call it heaven as you will see,*
> *A joyful place of peace and harmony.*[3]

As we waited our turn to scoop up steaming rice and zucchini, Arlane introduced me to Joshua and Luke. Joshua boasted a head of wiry, black hair, a bubble-shaped red nose and large, warm, intense eyes. He grabbed my hand and squeezed it like a juice orange; so did Luke. They were sharp, jovial young guys, inquisitive and amiable. And I soon felt comfortable and right at home with them.

As we shuffled around the coffee table we swapped backgrounds. Arlane, Joshua, Luke and his sister Christine had all been students together at the University of Michigan in Ann Arbor. Christine received her master's in clinical psychology and later traveled to California where she met the Community. One by one, the others had come out to Berkeley to visit Christine and eventually joined the group.

Arlane and I squeezed down cross-legged onto an open patch of rug and balanced our plates and Dixie cups of Kool-aid in our laps. What impressed me about Arlane was how much she related on a heart level. I guess I sometimes found myself being too intellectual. Her sense of fun, giggles and warm affection made her seem younger than her 28 years. When she laughed her large mouth sprang into a gorgeous toothy smile, her eyes sparked and her nose puckered. Sometimes she laughed so hard her shoulders jiggled.

Suddenly Arlane waved to a guy and girl standing in the vestibule, carrying books. "Hey Jacob, Sandra!" Minutes later the two student members squatted down next to us with plates piled high with food. Sandra Peters was a student in the Berkeley Law School. Jacob Gadon, a former third-year engineering student at the University of Pennsylvania, now majored in religious studies at Berkeley.

Sandra smiled a lot and looked like a plump Raggedy Ann with her blond pixie cut, knee-length dress, and enormous blue eyes magnified by Coke-bottle glasses.

Jacob displayed a more serious and studious appearance: coal-nugget eyes, attractively hooked nose and wire-rimmed glasses.

Somehow I felt drawn to the people of the Community. They were adventurous and philosophically minded, as I was. They talked about their travels, their anti-Vietnam War efforts, their investigation of different life-styles and philosophies—back-to-the-land organic farming, yoga, Thoreau and Buckminster Fuller. And with this talk my heart swelled with inspirations and my thoughts sailed off into golden worlds of realization—how rich and thrilling this thing called life!

The people I'd met so far seemed like such sincere, caring people, interested in me as a person and in what I wanted to do with my life. Talking came so easy. I looked around and saw that everyone was as much at ease as I was. We seemed to be in the company of people who cared, who listened intently to our every word.

As the four of us sat wedged in this pulsating room of young humanity, sharing our hopes, dreams, philosophies and intents, I felt myself being swept away in an intoxicating and exhilarating spirit of camaraderie.

After dinner the place rocked with guitar and Joshua's fiddle music, piano solos, singing trios, quartets and chorus lines. I was feeling so comfortable and self-confident that I picked up a guitar and ground out a tune from one of my music heroes, Bob Dylan, "I Shall Be Released." It didn't sound that great since my voice is pretty raspy and the guitar was a real cheapo, but when I sat down Luke slapped me on the back and Sandra, Arlane and others buried me in praises and applause as if I'd performed a magnificent Tchaikovsky number. I bathed in undivided attention and compliments that entire night, and I can't say I didn't enjoy it.

Dr. Durst, an English professor at a local college, delivered an impressive introductory lecture. Apparently "The Principles of Education" or "The Principles" for short comprised the foundation for their community effort, which was officially entitled "The New Education Development."

Dr. Durst paced around an easel full of colorful charts, gestured dynamically and occasionally set off a rumble of laughter with a humorous comment or anecdote.

"Just as scientific laws and principles govern the physical universe, so do certain laws and principles govern and dictate order in the internal or spiritual universe." He spoke eloquently, and through his voice and facial expressions he reached out and touched the audience with his sincerity and frankness. That our lecturer was a college professor lent a great deal of credibility and legitimacy to the philosophy he presented. Arlane mentioned that Durst had worked with the famed late psychologist Abraham Maslow.

At one point the professor meshed the fingers of both hands, hunched his back, and peered out through his fingers as if they were a thick wall pierced by a few peepholes. He explained how men, in coming to an understanding of life, view life and the world through a thick mesh of partial viewpoints. "Rather, we need to realize an all-encompassing, universal viewpoint of life." Then he swung his arms out wide like a great eagle embracing the sky.

To illustrate how men hold such partial viewpoints Durst related the well-known story of the king who requested five blind men to identify an object standing in his court—an elephant. Each blind man grasped a different limb or part of the animal and each perceived a different object. None of them could perceive "the whole elephant," as Durst called it.

I assumed Durst was suggesting the possibility of a more complete understanding of life. In any case, his anecdote diminished my somewhat skeptical attitude. I realized I might reject some valuable ideas if I clung to my own "partial" understanding of reality.

The lecture ended and Durst received a storm of applause. Although I found their philosophy interesting and was impressed by its spirit of good will, the professor's overview hadn't revealed much of anything about the specific purposes and objectives of the group. About all I'd learned was that "The Principles" were an eclectic yet ingenious and apparently logical arrangement of concepts from Judeo-Christianity, Taoism (specifically the concept of yin and yang) as well as various utopian and humanitarian philosophies.

Still, I *was* impressed by the spirit of the ideology. It fostered such positive notions as unity between races and nations, and harmony between man's individual and collective purposes such that men's actions would serve and benefit mankind as well as themselves. But if I wanted to learn the salient details, the real meat of their philosophy and group purposes, I'd probably have to attend the advanced lectures I'd heard about.

Blossom chattered gaily through a slide show of the Ideal City Project in Booneville, the weekend workshops and the group's maintenance and gardening companies. A lively refreshment hour followed: coffee, tea, punch, homemade cookies and brownies, cocktail party circles of conversation and laughter. A girl came by with a stack of applications for that weekend's workshop. I told her I'd have to give it some thought.

At 9:30 Joshua and Luke came strumming and singing Roy Roger's old farewell ballad, "Happy trails to you." And the guests were eased out the door as they chatted on and on, most of them not really wanting to leave.

"Sure, I'd love to. I'll be here tomorrow at six," I replied when Arlane invited me back for dinner the next evening. Then I floated out on the street inside a warm, glowing bubble of inspiration. Already I was looking forward to another pleasant evening of good food and conversation. Never had I met so many enthusiastic, idealistic people in one place, people with great hopes and ideals, people dedicated towards doing something positive in the world.

Chapter Four

The Family

*"Beware of false prophets, who come
to you in sheep's clothing but inwardly
are ravenous wolves," Matthew 7:15.*

I went to dinner and lecture every night that week until I'd heard nearly all of the lectures in the "Principles of Education." And I soon learned that the group didn't confine itself to the community-oriented programs which Blossom and Arlane had outlined when I first met them on Sproul Plaza. Lectures such as the "Principle of Creation" put forth a proof of the existence of God as well as of the existence of a "spiritual world."

Despite a few periods of teenage agnosticism I had basically believed there was a good Creator, a God. I'd attended Catholic schools for eight of my twelve years of education. But my religious upbringing had been fairly nominal. I'd never given the Bible much consideration, and like so many humans on this wide earth, only prayed in times of crises and dark despair. Accordingly, I could respect, perhaps even admire the Community's belief in God, even though this wasn't what originally attracted me to the group.

After each lecture I posed reams of questions to the lecturer and older members. But by Friday I still didn't know what made these people and their Community *tick*. There had to be something more to this group. What held them together? How could they maintain such incredible cohesiveness, or realize that tight, warm family spirit? Why and how could these people be so friendly and giving? What lay at the root? That's when I decided to accept Arlane's invitation to come to a workshop. It cost only $15. And since classes didn't start till Monday my weekend was homework-free.

At nine o'clock Saturday morning I walked into the Dana Street house living room carrying an old, green sleeping bag, toothbrush and shaving kit. The morning shone clean and fresh, casting sunlight on rows of metal folding chairs. I sat down and talked with Peter, a freshman engineering student who'd given me a ride home in his baby-blue '57 Chevy one evening.

Every few minutes other guests came ambling into the vestibule, and the members who'd invited them would shoot out of the living room to greet them.

By 9:30 twenty guests and twenty-five members were seated and waiting. Then Luke pranced in with his great smile, sunshine yellow shirt and brown tie. He welcomed us while one of the girls passed out songbooks.

"Let's clear the air of early morning sleepiness and grumpiness! We want to prepare ourselves so we can really receive Dr. Durst's message this morning!" Like a coach psyching up his team, he jabbed the air with a thin clenched fist.

With Christine drumming her guitar and Luke clapping in time, we started out with "You Are My Sunshine" and "There's a New World Coming". Then Christine yelled "Come on! Sing with your whole heart. I can't hear you!" So we all laughed and tried to sing with more gusto. We kept singing and clapping till an intoxicating frenzy of excitement and enthusiasm surged in the room. The last song, "Down by the Riverside," ended in a crescendo of whoops, howls and applause.

When Dr. Durst strode into the room a minute later I found myself riding an exhilarating high! And even though I'd heard Durst's introductory lecture before, I couldn't wait to hear what the professor had to say.

As he spoke, his eyes twinkled behind his gold-frame glasses. "Life is like a musical instrument in that it observes definite laws and principles which we must know in order to properly play it." Then he walked to the corner of the room and picked up a guitar. "Now if I don't know the principles of music, and specifically guitar music, I won't be able to produce harmonious sounds." He began strumming the open strings and it sounded like a three-year-old beating the guitar with a spatula. In time with his strum he sang, "Blue suede shoes, blue suede shoes, don't you step on my blue suede shoes." Laughter rolled through the room.

About 20 minutes into the lecture a blond-haired guy in front of me raised his hand but Dr. Durst ignored him. A minute later the lecturer paused to rearrange the charts on the easel. "Excuse me, Dr. Durst, how do you define 'ego'? I'm somewhat confused by the way you're using the term."

Looking very annoyed Dr. Durst snapped, "Please save your questions till after the lecture." Some of the members looked even more outraged than the professor, as if the poor guy had interrupted the mouthpiece of God! Then the lecture continued as if nothing had happened and soon the crowd was laughing and responding as before. And from that point on, not a soul peeped another question during the lectures.

People did fall asleep though; only God knows why at ten o'clock in the morning. Occasionally, a member's chin would sink into his or her chest as if someone had pulled a robot's electric plug. I'd observed the same sleep problem at the evening lectures; only then I'd assumed that the cause was a hard day's work.

A brief question-and-answer period followed the lecture, after which Luke announced that everyone had been assigned to one of the discussion groups. My group gathered in a far corner over Styrofoam cups of coffee and tea. The guests were Peter Norchrist, the engineering student, Gary Johnson, a student from Ontario, and myself. The community members were Joshua, Stefan Helengas, Jim Arle and Daniel Silverman. Daniel, a robust, jet-haired man of 24, led us in a discussion of the introductory lecture; he was at times funny and jovial, at others his walnut eyes flashed with warm concern.

Before the "Creation Lecture" Christine and Luke sent us reeling through some more clap and hammer-down songs. I had never seen a group of people who sang with such force and enthusiasm. And by the time Dr. Durst showed up I was feeling a definite buzz, as if I and the entire crowd were enveloped in a bubble of euphoria. The questions which had been mulling in my head from the discussion period were now replaced by the rosy bliss of being in the midst of such kind, cheerful and enthusiastic people. Again, with great eagerness I looked forward to Dr. Durst's presentation, as if he were going to reveal some profound secret, a novel cosmic formula which would explain the origin of all the love and good cheer which seethed around me. (The creation lecture essentially set forth the ultimate ideal of creation, a reality where the individual, family, nation and world are completely centered on God.)

After applauding Durst's second lecture we piled into a bunch of cars and drove to a park in the Bay Area hills. A winding 15-minute drive brought us to a cozy field encircled by hills of pine and eucalyptus trees. Seconds later an old farm truck pulled up with a dozen jumping, giggling workshoppers in the back. Then everyone swarmed onto the field and surrounded a checkered tablecloth stacked with paper plates, cups, napkins, baloney and cheese sandwiches, oranges, apples, carrots and oatmeal cookies.

By this time I was well acquainted with many group members along with some of the regular guests. I jostled and joshed around the mountain of food, feeling very much at home—snapping up sandwiches and fruit, sharing handshakes, backslaps and sunny comments. Maybe I felt so much at ease because we all seemed to share the same philosophical interests and untarnished hope and idealism. Somehow I felt I had known these people for years—or had it been all my life?

As our group sat in the warm grass, munching carrots and sandwiches, Daniel led a discussion of the morning lectures. There was something incredibly inspiring about this person. In the first place, he came through as a fiercely courageous and competent man. Yet it was more his capacity for love and compassion, and his ability to inspire others to develop this same capacity within themselves which drew me to him. A remarkable guy. Two years ago he'd graduated from the University of Pennsylvania and then gone West to visit his good friend Jacob Gadon. Jacob had moseyed west a year before Daniel and was already living with the Family by this time. Now, Daniel worked as an environmental engineer.

"I think it would be valuable to share our backgrounds and reasons for being here this weekend," said Daniel. "Could you start us out, Jim?"

Jim Arle spoke about his college days, how he'd majored in political science and graduated from the University of Wisconsin at Madison. He'd worked and traveled awhile. Then after six months, while passing through Berkeley, he met "the Family." Here he found something he had always been looking for. "Wow. I couldn't believe a group like this actually existed. Almost everywhere you go, people are only looking out for themselves. But these folks first thought about how they could best serve and love the other guy. Such an attitude of joyful living, of giving everything to each other and to God was very impressive."

Both Joshua and Stefan described their lives before encountering the community as periods of investigation, travel and search, while admitting that they never consciously realized they were searching at all. And just as Jim had done, each one talked about discovering "the Family" as if it were the pot of gold at the end of the rainbow.

Then it was Peter's turn. I liked the lanky, beak-nosed Yankee and his cutting sense of humor and critical mind. He seemed quite set in his ways for an 18-year-old. Already, he'd pretty much determined his career and life plans—engineering, and he was engaged to be married to a girl back in his home state of Massachusetts. An interesting blend of conservatism on the one hand and piercing insight and philosophical imagination on the other. He always wore these dark slacks and silver-buckled black loafers. Lanky built. Medium-length locks of somewhat greasy blond hair framed an intelligent, whitish face and a beak nose. I couldn't believe it when he cast his life's story in the same pattern and format as the others. He spoke in mystical, almost fatalistic terms of how he must have met the Community because there was something he had to learn from the Family. I guess the sharing session had drawn out his philosophical rather than his critical nature.

When my turn came it was difficult not to pattern my story after everyone else's. It seemed as if the group was saying, "You can say anything you want about the Family, just as long as it's positive." They were *expecting* me to make my previous life sound like a dreary search, and now that I'd found the Family I could hoot and howl for joy and never have another worry.

Instead I quickly summed up my most recent experiences:

graduated in three years from a Jesuit high school in Rochester, New York, then spent a wonderful year at a Dutch high school in Amsterdam, toured Europe in the summer, then came out to Berkeley.

Gary Johnson had this beautiful head of shaggy blond hair, and could strike this great philosophical pose. When his turn came to "share," as the members called it, he scratched his bearded chin, his eyes narrowed and gazed off into oblivion, "Hmmmmm."

The 24-year-old had studied mechanical engineering at the University of Western Ontario in London, Ontario. "After my third year I burned out and decided I needed a break," said Gary. In a blinding January snowstorm he began hitchhiking the long trek to California.

What he liked about the Community was the communal life-style. For a while now he'd been interested in communal living. Gary impressed me as a thoughtful and sensitive young man who had experienced a great deal in his lifetime.

I'd never seen a game played with such enthusiasm and insane fanatacism. The Family called it "spiritual dodge ball." The ball scorched back and forth across the line separating the two teams. When a player was hit a shuddering cry rose up as if a great general had been shot off his horse. The casualties stood on the sidelines and chanted, "Un-Ga-Wa! Un-Ga-Wa! Crushers got the power!" or some other chant to inspire their teams. Their fists pistoned in time.

It was sort of amusing to see college-age folks, graduates and people in their mid-twenties jumping and screaming like summer camp fifth-graders. Some moments I felt like a complete fool for participating; at others I was in awe of the members' enthusiasm for life and of the emotion that gushed around me.

Back at Dana Street, Dr. Durst resumed the lecture series with "The Cause of Crime." During the post-lecture discussion a new guest came into our group. Later I overheard Jim asking Joshua about him and why he'd joined our group so late. "Oh, he and his buddy were having negative give-and-take and multiplying a lot of doubt, so Luke split them up."

After the usual euphoric singing session Dr. Durst laid into "The Purpose of Mankind" lecture. Mankind's purpose was to realize perfect men and women, perfect families, and thereby realize perfect societies, nations and a perfect world.

I asked several questions during Durst's question-and-answer periods and many during the group discussions. And Joshua, Arlane and others would comment, "Wow, that's a *really* good question!" And they'd tell me how intelligent and perceptive I was. More often than not their answers were vague and elusive or they said, "Oh yeah. That question will be answered in the next lecture," or "in tomorrow's lectures."

As for the compliments on how smart and marvelous I was, they never stopped. But the members seemed so sincere. And their compliments made me feel good about myself. And even when their complimenting seemed artificial it didn't bother me much. Rather, I respected these efforts as attempts to create good will and a sense of community.

Before dinner a dense circle of sunny faces huddled around the coffee table. The smell of hot fish and rice poured in from the kitchen. I was glad the lectures had ended. My head swirled with the notions and ideological concepts of a full day of lecture and discussion. Suddenly Christine hoisted a lecture chart into view—a diagram of a great blue-green earth.

"I want you to envision this earth and really believe that we can change it, that we can make it a better world!" Thundering cheers and yahoos. "Do you believe you can?!"

The crowd boomed, "YES!"

"We can restore this world. Do you believe that? Do you believe we can restore this world?!"

"YES!"

The white Amazon towered beside the skinny Luke. When Christine's guitar began shuddering under her strum, arms locked around shoulders and the weave of bodies began swaying like a snow fence in March winds. Then the words of a Family song, a composition whose meaning was becoming more clear, reverberated in the room.

> Gonna build a Kingdom in this sad old land.
> Gonna build a Kingdom, it's at hand.

••

> Fight hard to gain the victory
>   to triumph for all men.
> We'll work to change this troubled world
>   all suffering to end.
> His kingdom we shall build with our
>   sweat and tears and blood.
> We'll smash to hell this hell on earth
> And make a new earth for God![4]

I hung between Gary and Joshua, swaying in a half-drunk euphoria. Gary caught my glance and we grinned crazily. This whole business about restoring the world seemed pretty flaky. Yet, as the last verses boomed, I thought: *You know, if this amazing spirit got big and strong enough, maybe it could change the world!*

Then Christine bowed her head and prayed for unity in the world. "O heavenly Father, we pray for the realization of one great family under you, one family under God."

During dinner Daniel had us work out a skit for evening entertainment. Although every group's skit turned out funny or entertaining, they all employed the same theme: lives of trouble and search which ultimately encounter the pot of gold at the end of the rainbow—the Family.

For the most part, Sunday's program followed Saturday's format—long lectures, singing sessions and group discussions all day.

During the dodge ball game Peter wanted to take a walk by himself in the park. But Daniel wanted him to stay with the group. Daniel had taken Peter aside and finally persuaded him to just hang around near the sidelines and watch.

In fact this was a main drawback about the workshop. From the minute we'd walked into the Dana Street house on Saturday morning, none of us had any time alone, not even a minute. All activity was group activity, and I had a hunch that Joshua was an assigned partner of sorts. Not that I minded his company; he was a super guy. But for the past two days he'd been glued to me like a diver's wet suit—always sitting next to me during lectures, discussions and meals; he slept next to me on the floor; he even went to the bathroom with me! I'd sit there on the pot and Joshua would stand outside the stall and rattle on and on about how great life in the Family was.

Durst closed the lecture series at 5:30 that Sunday night with "The Consummation of Human History." And the workshop crowd shook the walls and floors with applause for the charming and brilliant professor.

When we gathered to sing before dinner Luke made an announcement. He thanked all us "wonderful people" for attending the workshop. "And if you want to find out if the way we live is a true way of life, you're welcome to move in for however long you'd like and learn for yourself."

Our spaghetti dinner was not the precious asylum of relaxation I'd longed for. Our group had just started slurping the rich spaghetti when Daniel broke in, "Well, what kind of skit shall we work out for tonight, guys?" Groan.

After the skits, Christine, Jessica and Big Al gave their testimonies. When Big Al lumbered to his feet he looked like a black bear rising up on his hindlegs. Even his huge stocking feet looked like bear paws.

Al explained that after he got his physics degree he decided he needed a rest from the academic scene. So he set off to travel. "By the time I met Blossom I'd been traveling for a year. The workshop turned out to be one of the most wonderful experiences of my life. It truly enlightened me about the meaning and purpose of life, and I came to love everyone here so much."

Instead of turning his head, he stiffly swiveled his whole body from side to side. Big Al had decided after a week that it was time to move on to other experiences, and to practice what he'd learned from the Family. "I'll never forget the night I was getting ready to leave. Joshua told me, 'Al, sometimes you have to sacrifice something small to gain something very great and valuable.' But I told Joshua I couldn't stay."

With 50 pairs of eyes glued on the big bear, Al described how a strange thing happened as he packed his things. "A strap tore loose when I packed up my backpack. I tried again and then the whole thing just fell apart." Al reproduced his look of astonishment and everyone laughed. "That's when I started thinking. 'Maybe someone's trying to tell me something!' "

Al decided to stay with the Family a little longer. Along with

answers to many of his questions about life he had discovered a
unique and meaningful way of living. When he finished we
clapped furiously. I could well relate to his feelings about the
need for purpose and meaning for our daily lives.

Then a guest with a bowl-shaped mop of black hair sat on
his haunches and raised his hand. Al nodded. "I just wanted to
mention something," said the guest. "This weekend has been
an amazing and wonderful experience. But everything that's
been said so far doesn't seem to explain what makes this whole
thing possible." He spoke with pleading, outstretched hands.
"There must be something more to all this. I just *feel* it." The
membership roared. I wondered what they were laughing at. I
admired this guy's courage for pointing out this aspect of the
workshop which I'd sensed all along.

The entire weekend I'd looked to the lectures and the membership for an answer to my question—"What keeps the Family
together; how can they live such lives of serving and caring?"
But I could never extract any real explanations or answers from
the members. And the lecture series, although interesting and
thought-provoking, remained for me a vague and noncommit-
tal conglomeration of utopian philosophy.

But Al grinned stupidly and looked to the staff members for
support. Luke strode to the rescue. "Many of these kinds of
questions will be answered at the 'Advanced Workshop' next
week." Luke clasped his hands and smiled serenely.

That night, Gary Johnson decided to move in with the
Family, along with three other guests. He'd give the Family a try
to see what it was like. Besides, he had other good reasons for
sticking around—he'd run out of money and had no place to
stay. And Berkeley seemed like an ideal place to spend the
winter. Joshua whooped at the news; Daniel and Jim mauled
Gary with hugs and backslaps. "Welcome to the Family!"

For me the workshop had been amusing, enjoyable and
inspiring, but I had no desire to commit myself to anything. I
wanted to *learn* from the Family, not join it. I was enjoying my
life as a college student and wanted very much to remain free to
explore the exciting Berkeley student community. Besides, I
felt I had to know a lot more about this intriguing organization.
I said good-bye to Gary, Daniel, Arlane and everyone and
walked the 10 blocks back to my dorm.

Chapter Five

Unification Church

*"It were a journey like
the path to heaven,"
Milton Comus 1.303.*

At 9:00 A.M. of the morning after the workshop I sat in my first Afro-American English Comp class. Professor Eli Pell wore an African dashiki and matching cap of silky, shouting reds, blacks and greens, and came off as a sophisticated Dick Gregory—funny, mellow, provocative.

Yet somehow I felt surprisingly detached from the class and the collegiate world it represented. My consciousness still drifted in the euphoria and excitement of the Family's weekend workshop. I couldn't stop pondering the endless possibilities and potential of a group that possessed such amazing spirit and enthusiasm.

Professor Pell talked about black folklore and literature, new literary movements as products of new civil rights movements and other contemporary political movements. It was all so foreign, so different from the world of my friends back at the New Education Development: coldly intellectual, lacking in hope and moving inspiration. I looked around the room and almost felt sorry for the other students, most of whom seemed bored or apathetic. In discovering the Family, I believed I had found a unique and exceptional source of knowledge and inspiration. Although I was surprised at my own haughtiness, I felt that for all intents and purposes I was the only one in the class who was really with it.

That first week I didn't have much homework so I stopped

over at the Family's for several evening programs, not so much for the lectures as for the pleasant company and leisurely dinner.

And every night Peter and I would hop in his shiny blue Chevy and cruise dorm-wards along Telegraph Avenue. I liked the crazy Yankee, and we got along well. The focus of our conversations always returned to the Family and followed a certain pattern, a constant switching back and forth between discussing positive and negative aspects of the group—pro, con, pro, con.

Peter heaved on his cigarette and flicked the ashes out the window. "You know, I'm not much interested in their ideology. It's the spirit of the group that really impresses me." Then we talked about people like Daniel and Luke and their impressive determination to love, serve and grow; how their example had expanded our awareness of our own capabilities and potential. Peter swerved off Telegraph towards his dorm. A gust of warm night air flashed my face.

"What bugs me though is the way Christine runs things sometimes," said Peter. "She can be a real drill sergeant. Lyn is in Christine's trinity (the Family was divided into 'trinities,' subgroups of five to eight members with one 'trinity leader'); and Christine is always telling her how to dress, how to wear her hair, even how to brush her teeth—Christine thinks there's a heavenly way to do *everything!*"

"Talk about going overboard," I said, "Fred was like a live wire after that job with the Family maintenance crew. They cleaned carpets for two straight days without sleeping; singing and gulping coffee and cookies to stay awake."

I always walked away from these discussions with a jumble of conflicting feelings along with a desire to go back to the center to learn more, to understand exactly what this deal was all about.

Arlane had been asking me all week to go to the Advanced Workshop. And Thursday I did sign up. Then I found out that the "Advanced Workshop" was actually a presentation of the main body of Family doctrine—"The Divine Principle." The Principles of Education had just been a simplified and quite watered-down version of the Divine Principle; and this adapted version had been written by a Mr. Choi to appeal to the liberal tastes and values of the West Coast.

I also learned that the Family was in fact a national and worldwide organization, well established not only in the United States, but also in Europe, Japan and Korea. Its official name—"The Holy Spirit Association for the Unification of World Christianity," or "Unification Church" for short.

Thursday night I worked with the Family's maintenance company. This was a customary way of paying for the workshop if a guest couldn't or preferred not to pay cash. So from midnight till six in the morning I worked with Joshua's crew cleaning the Victoria Station restaurant in San Francisco.

The Brothers (as all male Family members were called) worked furiously scrubbing kitchen slats, sweeping floors and vacuuming eerie box-car dining rooms filled with the ghost smells of cigarettes and liquor. To keep their morale up they sang medleys of songs, either individually or in unison. I'd never seen any group of human beings work with such energy and joy. Their joy was refreshing in contrast with the attitude of so many people in society who view their work with apathy or resentment.

"Do everything with your whole heart," said Joshua. "And be everyday joyful—that's what our Onni tells us. If you give your 100 percent, time will fly, you'll do a job you can be proud of, and you'll come to love and enjoy your work." Now and then the Brothers let go a gutsy cheer they'd learned from Onni—"One-actualize! Two actualize! Three-actualize! One-Oh-Oh!"

I had heard a lot about this Korean woman. In 1970 she had founded the Oakland center. They spoke of her as if she were a saint, a shining whirlwind of holy energy and goodness. I was looking forward to meeting her so I could find out what all the fuss was about.

Chapter Six

Divine Principle

"A goodly apple rotten at the heart.
O, what a goodly outside falsehood hath!"
William Shakespeare, Merchant of Venice.

It was a rich, clear Saturday morning in early October. Peter, Gary, myself and two dozen other workshoppers were sitting in the second-floor lecture room of the Regent Street House. Outside the open windows, great elms creaked against the sky, and a gentle wind swept in the good smell of warm, brown leaves.

Blossom and Cherie started out the workshop with a rip-roar of Family songs. "Sing out with your whole heart!" said bubbly, plump Cherie. "We want to prepare the spiritual atmosphere and really open our hearts so we can receive the message of this first lecture."

I didn't know what they meant by "spiritual atmosphere," but the singing sure "opened my heart." When I first sat down I was still viewing the world through my grumpy, early morning spectacles, magnifiers of bleakness and suspicion. When the last strum of Cherie's guitar faded out I felt carefree, slightly soaring.

Then Blossom bowed her head and began to pray. "O dear Father! *Dear* heavenly Father! Thankyousooooomuch heavenly Father for bringing these wonderful Brothers and Sisters together here today. We *pray* we can open our hearts to receive these precious words which Daniel will share with us now. . . ."

Meanwhile Arlane had squeezed her face shut and was softly pounding her knee. Other members were doubled over in their seats muttering, "Oh *please* heavenly Father! Oh *yes* heavenly Father!"

Then Blossom closed her prayer. "Thankyousooooomuch heavenly Father for your precious words. We pray all these things in our Master's name."

The fervent praying startled me. In the course of the past two weeks, what I had first thought was a community service group had gradually revealed itself to be an intensely religious-spiritual venture. At the open-house dinners Luke had asked for "a few moments of silent meditation." Now they were praying in quivering, high-pitched voices as if their lives hung by kite string over a pool of crocodiles. Although by now I'd come to admire the members' faith in God, the present level of fervor and emotion was a bit too much for me! And what did Blossom mean by "our Master"? I assumed it referred to Jesus.

The Principle of Creation

Suddenly our lecturer, Daniel Silverman, swept to the front of the room in his three-piece suit. As he arranged his black three-ring binder on the wooden lectern he scanned the audience. "The purpose of religion is to enable man to overcome his internal ignorance while the purpose of science is to enable man to overcome his external ignorance. The Bible has always been a guidebook to the truth or to the knowledge of God. In the course of civilization, man's spirit and intellect have developed. Therefore the guidebook to the truth must also develop in its expression."

Daniel picked up a piece of chalk and scratched out three terms on the blackboard:

OLD TESTAMENT   NEW TESTAMENT   NEW REVELATIONS

"Today's philosophies and religions have just about lost their ability to lead man to a life of goodness, to God." Daniel shook a pointed finger above his head. This comment instantly struck a chord in me. The Catholic church and most organized religions impressed me as stuffy institutions that lacked the zing and vitality needed to really inspire men to live for others and for God. "Therefore, if God does indeed exist He must reveal a new and higher expression of truth in order to bring all men to Him and realize this life of goodness."

Silverman quoted from the Gospel of John to support the

idea that a higher expression of truth must come. Here Jesus says, "I have yet many things to say to you, but you cannot bear them now. When the Spirit of truth comes, he will guide you into all the truth" (John 16:12,13).*

When Daniel finished with this introduction he erased the blackboard and launched into his lecture on the "Principle of Creation." "Mankind has never understood the true meaning of life, or the purpose of the universe," said Daniel. "And this ignorance will end when man finally knows the fundamental principle through which God created the universe and the human race." Silverman was sweeping an intense look through the room as members scribbled hurriedly in their notebooks.

Daniel then went into a discussion on the nature of God and the world of creation. "All things, from man to the atom, possess dual characteristics of internal character and external form as well as dual characteristics of male and female or positive and negative. These dual characteristics are part of God's own nature and were projected by Him into all creation.

"So what was God's original motivation for creating man and the universe?" boomed Daniel rhetorically. He explained that God needed an object to reflect His love and His very nature so that He could experience joy, just as an artist derives joy from seeing his very self reflected in his own artwork. "But God can experience the fullest joy only through man since man was created in the very image of God, while the physical universe is only symbolic of God."

With every new concept Daniel chalked the blackboard with a table or diagram reminiscent of high school chemistry—circles, connecting arrows, positive and negative signs. This approach lent a scientific aura to the Family's "Principles."

Daniel then explained what apparently were two all-important and central Divine Principle themes: (1) the subject-object relationship, and (2) the "Four Position Foundation." By now I'd noticed that one fundamental theme permeated Family doctrine, namely the concept of dualities—yin-yang, positive-negative, internal-external, male-female, etc.

It turned out that this concept of universal duality found its

---

* *In its context it becomes clear that the "Spirit of the truth" refers to the Holy Spirit who came shortly after Jesus spoke these words.*

basis in the Divine Principle's subject-object relationship—all beings and all things can exist only through the reciprocal give-and-take relationship of its subject and object parts. For instance, man is composed of men and women, animals of male and female; plants involve stamen and pistil; molecules are composed of positive and negative ions, and the simplest atom of a proton and electron.

Silverman then sketched four circles in a diamond arrangement. He labeled the top point of the diamond "God," the bottom point "New Creation," and the two outer points "subject" and "object." This represented the Four Position Foundation. It expressed how God relates to man and all creation, as well as the ultimate *purpose* of creation.

THE FOUR POSITION FOUNDATION

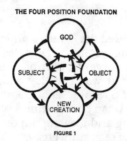

FIGURE 1

"When a subject and object are united through give-and-take action and then form unity with God, a new being, a new object to God is formed." Daniel used the ideal state of man to illustrate the Four Position Foundation. Men and women would mature and marry realizing object positions to God (the ultimate subject) and also producing a third object position through their offspring.

THE FOUR POSITION FOUNDATION
IN THE CASE OF MANKIND

FIGURE 2

Then stabbing his blackboard diagram with a piece of chalk, Daniel boomed, "So in the ideal world of creation, all things will be involved in four position foundations centered on God; and all positions will enjoy reciprocal relationships of subject and object."

THE IDEAL WORLD OF
GOD'S SOVEREIGNTY

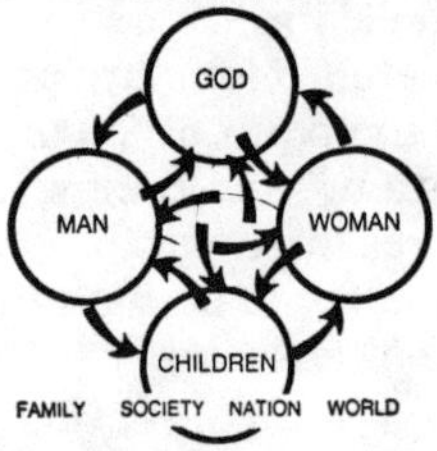

GOD

MAN   WOMAN

CHILDREN

FAMILY   SOCIETY   NATION   WORLD

FIGURE 3

Up till now I'd viewed the Family's philosophy as just that, a philosophy, a guiding system of principles and values. Nothing earthshaking. Every organization had some sort of guiding philosophy whether it was the Boy Scouts, the Knights of Columbus, or the U.S. State Department.

But our lecturer wasn't presenting a philosophy. Gone was Dr. Durst's sweeping and glowing philosophical prose on the approaching unity of mankind, etc., etc. As Daniel strode back and forth, slapping the lectern and scrawling earnestly on the blackboard, his voice rose and fell from bellows to urgent whispers. And it finally dawned on me that he wasn't presenting an "interesting philosophy" but rather a powerful system of teachings which the Family viewed as essential and eternal truths. This realization brought on a burning queasiness—I had become involved in something bigger than I'd originally perceived.

At that point I borrowed some paper and a pen and began taking notes. Afterwards, when I had more time, I would thoroughly examine their ideology and give it the third degree.

After a few humorous comments to lighten up the atmosphere Daniel began explaining the nature of the spiritual world. "Man is the mediator between the spiritual and physical worlds."

I did believe that man consisted of both spirit and body. But Daniel went quite a bit further and asserted that man lived simultaneously in the physical and spiritual worlds. Man couldn't *perceive* the spiritual world around him because his spiritual senses had been severely dulled and in most cases were lost due to the fall of man.

My discussion group leader was a bony-faced, wimpy-looking guy named Isaiah Reez. Every few minutes his trousers would slide down over his skeleton hips; then he'd tug them back up. But the force of his keen mind made you forget about his wimpy appearance and slight lisp.

"Most people have a very external concept of perfection," said Isaiah. "Some think Jesus never spilled a speck of food in His life. Perfection is rather a state where you are one with God's desires, one with God's *heart.*"

Isaiah began poking a bony finger at his chest. "In this state of oneness with God you would never commit an evil act because you would instantly share the intense pain and sorrow God would feel because of that act."

Jim Arle was in my discussion group again, only this time as my spiritual partner. Suddenly he burst out, "A world of men and women all one with heavenly Father's heart! What possibilities! No more murder, war or oppression. A world where God's love shines like sunlight and unites all people and all nations! A human family in tune with nature!"

At first I was taken aback by Jim's outburst. The whole idea of perfection seemed flaky and unrealistic. But I got to thinking about how Isaiah had defined perfection, not as a state where one couldn't make mistakes, but rather as a oneness with the desires of God. Could this kind of perfection be man's ultimate destination?

I began toying with the mind-boggling possibilities: men forever motivated by vast love instead of profits; people united to eliminate hunger, poverty and exploitation. What incredible possibilities might result from such a perfection—an almost absurd concept, but no more absurd I thought than the recent carnage in Vietnam or the suffering of the world's sick and poor.

The Fall of Man
After Cherie offered an almost tearful prayer, Daniel Silver-

man manned the lectern. The hurgle-burgle stopped instantly and all eyes converged on the young engineer-executive. He moved around the lectern, ominously, like a sorcerer. The members seemed different too. They sat erect with somber looks as if they were bracing themselves for a scolding they knew they deserved.

The sorcerer jerked his head up to face the room. "God's highest expression of Himself, and His most precious creation, was the first man and woman, Adam and Eve." Silverman then restated God's original ideal. Initially, Adam and Eve were spiritually immature and related only as Brother and Sister. They were meant to grow to perfection, become husband and wife and, through their offspring, realize God's kingdom of heaven on earth.

A thundercloud look flashed in Daniel's eyes. "Yet we know from the story of Genesis that God's ideal was shattered by the fall of Adam and Eve. For centuries Christians and Jews have believed that the transgression was an act of disobedience, the eating of a literal fruit. To this day, what actually happened in the Garden of Eden has remained a mystery."

THE FALLEN WORLD OF
SATAN'S SOVEREIGNTY

FIGURE 4

The lecturer asserted that no loving father would have damned his children to millenniums of suffering because of a simple act of disobedience. Clearly, the forbidden fruit was not a literal fruit. Then, through a detailed argument of Bible quotes, Daniel finally concluded that the tree of life symbolized perfected Adam and the tree of the knowledge of good and evil symbolized perfected Eve. Then he pointed out that Adam and Eve had been naked and unashamed prior to the Fall, and had covered their lower parts with fig leaves *after* the Fall. Suddenly Daniel raised a fist and thundered, "As it is the nature of man to conceal an area of transgression, it is clear that Adam and Eve were ashamed of their lower parts because they committed *sin* through them!"

I was impressed by the barrage of Bible quotes, although admittedly I didn't know the Bible very well. And there *was* a certain logic to his argument. Then I noticed not everyone followed the lecture as closely as I did. A few Brothers and Sisters were nodding off into various stages of drugged sleep. Poor Joshua leaned closed-eyed and open-mouthed over the chair's lip at such a precarious angle I was afraid he was going to fall on his ear. Occasionally, a member sitting next to a sleep victim would haul away and send a fist crashing into a slouching back or shoulder. It was an amusing/shocking freak show.

Daniel continued. He said God appointed Lucifer as teacher and servant to raise Adam and Eve. The archangel came to envy the father-child love Adam and Eve received from God, and he also began to lust after Eve—the beautiful daughter of God.

Somehow I was reacting to this bizarre lecture with fascination rather than with usual skepticism. I felt I was watching the unfolding of a prehistoric Shakespearean drama.

"Driven by lust and a desire to usurp Adam's position, Lucifer initiated an illicit sexual relationship with Eve!" Silverman's eyes now flashed righteous anger. He declared that this act constituted Lucifer's fall (where he became Satan) as well as the *spiritual* fall of man. Instantly Eve realized she had violated the purpose of creation and that *Adam* was her true spouse. She ran to Adam and seduced him, thinking this would restore her position to God. This act constituted the *physical* fall of man.

The air felt tense, live-wire electrified. Several Sisters sat bent over, clutching their faces. Daniel's head hung down and I thought I saw tears in his eyes.

"And God saw everything that happened. In anguish He cried out, 'No, Eve! Eve! Please don't do it!' . . . But Adam and Eve gave in to temptation. And by their premature sexual relationship they annihilated God's great hope for mankind." A Sister in the front row burst into fits of sobbing. Joshua, Arlane and others sat dejected and watery-eyed.

Daniel gripped the rim of the lectern. "God had poured out

every ounce of His energy and love into the creation of a beautiful universe for His perfect, happy children. He had such *great hopes* for His beloved children. But they were all shattered and His world was transformed into a pit of crime, immorality and suffering—centered not on Himself, but on *Satan!* Our heavenly Father's heart in every sense of the word was literally *broken!*"

By now entire rows were weeping or sobbing softly, even the Brothers. After an aching pause Daniel resumed in a low, tremulous voice: "Our blood is tainted by the hideous sin of our ancestors. And for six thousand years our heavenly Father has been cut off from us, suffering, crying, crying every day yearning for His children."

Daniel closed the lecture. Then Cherie prayed through gulping sobs and apologized to God for our fallen nature. "Don't worry, heavenly Father! We won't rest till we've healed your broken heart and brought all your children back to you!"

I had stopped taking notes a while ago and sat dumbfounded through the entire emotional episode. Thoughts battled: "Wow! Do they really believe this actually happened? It sounds so weird." Then later, "Man, I don't know, it *could* have been sexual. It kind of makes sense, like it could be more true than you think."

We stood up, slung arms over shoulders, and sang, "I'll Never Leave You Anymore," to the melody of the American folk song, "The Water Is Wide." Amidst the mournful tune, the swaying, and the ocean of sobs, I guess I really didn't know *what* to think.

The Principle of Restoration Through Indemnity

Daniel's last lecture for the day proclaimed that with the fall of man all was not lost. Through the Principle of Indemnity God planned to restore man to his original position before the Fall. Indemnity meant paying a fraction of our debt to God, which He in His forgiveness accepts as if it were full payment. Indemnity could be paid in many different ways: through prayer, faithfulness, fasting, physical suffering. Paying indemnity separates man from Satan and brings him closer to God's side. God *can't* restore man without his cooperation. In the realization of God's ideal, God has roughly a 95-percent portion of responsibility and man has roughly a five-percent portion of responsibility.

Our lecturer outlined how each major biblical character from Abel to Noah to Abraham had the mission of paying the required indemnity, thus laying the foundation for the coming of the Messiah, the second Adam. All these central figures failed to fully complete their missions. Finally, through Moses, the foundation for the coming of the Messiah was established on the national level (i.e. the "nation" of Israel).

Daniel closed this novel interpretation of Old Testament history with an announcement that Sunday's first lecture would discuss the coming of the second Adam, Jesus Christ.

The Mission of Jesus

My eyes fluttered open Sunday morning to see smiling Luke and Isaiah standing at the foot of my sleeping bag strumming guitars and singing, "You Are My Sunshine!" Compared to my buzzing alarm clock it seemed a nice way to wake up. Soon the field of male sleeping bags on the living room floor stirred, sprouted to attention and trotted off to the bathroom.

Minutes later Isaiah was leading the advanced workshoppers in schoolkids-type morning exercises, a "hokey-pokey" dance, and camp songs like "Zippadeedoodah." But the Family's crazy, energetic spirit was so contagious that these grammar school games seemed more entertaining than childish.

Dave and the lectern stood silhouetted in the morning sun which streamed through the window behind him. He began his lecture on "The Coming of the Messiah" with the question: "What was the purpose of the coming of Jesus?" Then Daniel quoted Matthew 5:48: "You, therefore, must be perfect, as your heavenly Father is perfect." Silverman concluded that Jesus' purpose in coming was to save fallen man, to realize in man the originally intended state of perfection.

"But what is the extent of the salvation Christians have through faith in the crucified Jesus?" Daniel explained that since Christians had in fact not achieved perfection, it was clear that man could not be completely saved through faith in Jesus alone.

The lecturer huddled over the black binder for a moment, then straightened himself. "We must now ask ourselves

whether the crucifixion of Jesus was the original predestina-
tion of God? John 1:11 reads, 'He came to his own home, and
his own people received him not.' "Then Silverman strafed the
room with a look of spears. "God wanted His chosen people, all
of Israel, to believe in and follow Jesus as Messiah. If it was
God's plan to simply send His Son to be crucified, as many
believe today, then why did He prepare the Jewish people for
over 4,000 years? Isn't it far more logical that God prepared the
children of Israel in order to *protect* His Son, to enable an evil
and disbelieving world to recognize and *accept* His Son instead
of killing Him as they killed the Old Testament prophets?"

According to the Divine Principle, one of Jesus' central
strategies consisted of winning over the Jewish leadership—
scribes, Pharisees, and high priests. But in the end, He could
only muster a band of uneducated laborers and fishermen.
Here Daniel boomed another quote from Matthew where Jesus
says: " 'O Jerusalem, Jerusalem, killing the prophets and ston-
ing those who are sent to you! How often would I have gathered
your children together as a hen gathers her brood under her
wings, and you would not!' " (Matt. 23:37).

Daniel Silverman's voice rose and dipped like some pas-
sionate swallow as he reeled off Bible quotes and described
Jesus' dismal situation. "No one truly believed in Him or supported Him: not His own brothers and sisters, nor His mother
and father, not even His disciples; and least of all not the
Jewish people and their leaders."

Speaking of support, Daniel wasn't getting much of it from
the row of members standing in the back. All of them fought
desperately to stay awake; swinging arms and pumping fists.
When Joshua nodded off Arlane would punch him in the shoulder. When Arlane nodded off, and if Joshua happened to be
awake, he would return the favor.

"Even John the Baptist failed Jesus and failed his mission
as forerunner," said Daniel. "John lacked faith in Jesus and
instead of uniting with Jesus as His chief disciple, he continued to preach independently."

Silverman chopped the air with an open hand. "John was
one of the most respected men in all of Israel, and his failure to
support Jesus prevented countless Jews from believing in
God's Son!" (Later I learned what a gross distortion of Scripture

was involved in this Unification Church interpretation of the mission of John the Baptist, as well as of the mission of Jesus.)

A sob broke the hush as the Sister in the front row began crying again. A cloud bank of sorrow had descended over the room; even Daniel's eyes looked slightly liquid. Somehow this new perspective of Jesus' life and mission seemed authentic and true the way Daniel explained it. As if this had all really happened.

Daniel Silverman walked out from behind the lectern. "We can now understand that the crucifixion of Jesus did not take place according to God's will. It was rather a crime which resulted from the ignorance, hardheartedness and disbelief of Jesus' own people." Silverman paused for several seconds, then declared, "The message is clear—Jesus did *not* come to die!"

Sudden skepticism jolted the spell I'd been under. A timeless belief, a rock in my Catholic upbringing had been violated. *Wait a minute!* I thought. *That's not what happened. . . . That's not the way I learned it!*

As our lecturer continued piling up more arguments and Bible quotations to support this teaching, I sat there in mild shock. *Jesus didn't come to die?! Why hadn't I seen what Daniel was leading up to?* And the funny thing was that Silverman's arguments had impressed me, and I'd even agreed with some of his conclusions. It was as if I'd fallen under the spell of his words—this missionary of mysteries. All along he'd been wooing us, pleading for our realization of some newly revealed "Divine Truth."

It had suddenly become apparent that the group I was involved with might not be as benign and wonderfully positive as I'd believed. I realized, *My God! I'd better be sure this isn't some kind of weird religious group!*

And in that moment I felt shadowed by a monster-image of the Family as a pernicious group of bizarre ideologues and religious fanatics. I'd been taking notes all along, occasionally scribbling questions in the margin. From that point on, the margins were crammed with doubt and skepticism.

Daniel had succeeded in whipping up an atmosphere of helpless, gnawing grief, a feeling that the past 2,000 years of bloodshed, atrocities and human suffering could have been avoided if only Israel had *accepted* Jesus of Nazareth instead of crucifying Him. The members' weeping over "the greatest tragedy of all time next to the Fall" gradually subsided as Silverman devoted the remainder of the lecture to an elaboration of Jesus' mission.

The Family's Christology viewed Jesus as a sinless babe of human parents who eventually grew to perfection. A perfect man but not God; although one with God, *not* God Himself.

The Divine Principle teaches that Jesus Christ came to marry a perfect mate, establish a perfect family and on that foundation realize the Kingdom of heaven on earth. In other words, He came as the second Adam to fulfill the mission which Adam and Eve had so miserably failed.

In fact, around 500 B.C. God sent sages and holy men—Malachi, Gautama Buddha, Confucius, and Socrates—to raise the level of heart and intellect among all people to enable the world to recognize and accept the coming Messiah. Jesus was to become spiritual ruler and Messiah—King first to the Roman Empire, and then to the entire world.

"Jesus' crucifixion," emphasized Daniel, "was only a secondary course and provided only spiritual salvation. When God's Son realized that Israel was not going to accept Him, He chose the only course available to Him. He took the cross as a condition of indemnity to accomplish at least spiritual salvation for mankind. And God relinquished Jesus' body to Satan as ransom. Christ's physical death on the cross represented the very act of Satan claiming Jesus' body. Thus the hope of physical salvation was squashed and man's blood remained tainted with sin, with satanic nature." (In refuting the bodily resurrection of Jesus, our speaker declared that it was Christ's very substantial "spirit man" which had appeared to the disciples after His death.)

Daniel sketched another diamond-shaped "four position foundation," saying that "Jesus was in the position of mankind's true father. Though He was never able to marry a perfect mate, spiritual salvation for mankind still required a true mother as well as a true father. God sent the Holy Spirit as our 'true mother.' "

Daniel Silverman closed the lecture like a poet finishing the reading of an epic poem, with reverence and hushed passion.

"Jesus was unable to establish God's kingdom on earth, and this is why God had to plan for a second coming of Christ. The Messiah, the Lord of the Second Advent, must come to complete God's purpose of creation."

The Consummation of Human History

As we were sitting down for the weekend's last lecture, "The Consummation of Human History," I asked Jim Arle what had happened to Jay, one of our guests. I hadn't seen him at the last couple group discussions.

"Oh, he got real skeptical, real negative. So we had to ask him to leave." Apparently, eliminating sharp questioners was one way they maintained group harmony.

When Daniel manned the lectern he didn't flash us his usual smile. Wrinkles lined his forehead: his eyes dark omens. "The spirit man can only grow to perfection through the physical body, through physical life on earth. Thus in order to accomplish man's physical salvation, the Messiah, the Lord of the Second Advent, must be born on earth in the flesh."

According to our workshop speaker, it was incomprehensible to the intellect of modern man that Christ would return on the clouds. He made it seem both irreligious and unscientific to accept historic Christian teachings regarding the second coming of Christ.

"In Luke 17:24,25 we read that Jesus said, in anticipation of the Second Coming, 'So will the Son of man be in his day. But first he must suffer many things and be rejected by this generation.' "* Daniel began fencing with his pointer finger. "But if the Lord is going to come on the clouds with angels blasting trumpets for all the world to see, who would dare persecute Him, or even want to? Clearly, Jesus predicted the coming Lord's persecution because Jesus knew that the Lord would be born a man and have to endure persecution before the world would accept Him."

At this point, Daniel plopped a large chart on the blackboard rim which exhibited three historical time lines, one above the other, respectively: the 2,000 biblical years from Adam to Abraham; the 2,000 years from Abraham to Jesus; and the 2,000 from Jesus to the present. Rattling off numerous

* *In its context the "Son of Man" refers to Jesus, not to a "Lord of the Second Advent."*

historical dates and periods, Silverman compared the 2,000 years of Judaic history before Christ to the 2,000 years of European history after Christ.

The 400 years of Jewish slavery in Egypt were compared to a supposed 400 years of early Christian persecution. Silverman continued drawing "history parallels" until he had reached the last time-block in the history time lines. The 400 years between the "great reformer" Malachi and the coming of Jesus Christ* lined up neatly with the 400 years between the great reformer Martin Luther and the present.

Then Daniel Silverman let the bomb drop: "Since God sent the Messiah 400 years after Malachi, He will again try to establish the Kingdom of God 400 years after the great reformer Martin Luther. And since Luther's greatest years were between 1517 and 1530 we can expect that the Lord of the Second Advent was born 400 years after Martin Luther, somewhere between 1917 and 1930.

It seemed eternities of seconds before it sunk in. *What!* I thought. *That means that the Messiah is alive right now! Holy Moses. So that's what Daniel's been leading up to this whole time.* And within that cascade of thought I realized that this was the Family's secret; this is what was behind it all—a messianic mission. This explained their intense enthusiasm, hope and incredible drive.

Yet I felt mixed emotions—revulsion at what sounded far-out, bizarre and dangerous, versus a cautious desire not to reject something which might, *just might* be true and good.

Silverman barreled through a discussion of where the Messiah would come from. He quoted Revelation 7:2: "Then I saw another angel ascend from the rising of the sun, with the seal of the living God." The "Principle" interpreted this as meaning that the Messiah would be born in the Far East—Korea, Japan or China. China and Japan were ruled out since China was a communist nation on the "satanic side," and Japan entered the period of the second advent as a totalitarian nation. "Therefore the nation where Christ will appear is Korea."

---

* *This historical period is quite fictitious. Old Testament scholars estimate that the prophet Malachi lived around 500 B.C. Also, the era of Christian persecution was far less than 400 years; for all intents and purposes it ended with the Roman emperor Constantine's conversion to Christianity and his Edict of Milan in A.D. 313.*

A young man in the back row suddenly piped in, "Who is the Messiah, or who do you think he is?"

Daniel paused, then said, "Well I have my own opinion. But I feel it's better if each person finds out and decides for himself."

We were left hanging on the thought that the Messiah was among the human race, walking the earth somewhere at that very moment. Some great man sent by God was about to try to bring in the kingdom of heaven. The purpose of creation, the task which God had tried to bring about since the fall of Adam and Eve—what Jesus had failed to accomplish—was now to be done, in our time.

I was dumbfounded. *Now? In our time?* It was an almost exhilarating thought. *On the other hand, couldn't this be some flaky operation?*

Everyone filed out of the room, through the stillness of thought, until only Daniel and I remained. I sat in the front row staring at the chart. It was clear that this was not the simple community of nice people I had thought it was, not the warm living experience where young folks practiced brotherhood and love. No, much more. A whole new way of viewing life and the purpose of our existence. But could it be? What was going on? What was happening to me? I sat there, with me staring at the chart, Daniel staring at me, and the chart staring out into a world that had been turned upside down. Honest to God, I just sat there not knowing *what* to think.

Chapter Seven

The Decision

*Yes, I'm being followed by a moon
shadow moon shadow—moon shadow,"
Cat Stevens, 1970.[5]*

That Sunday night the workshop crowd gathered at Dana Street for a curry-chicken dinner. As I stared into a pot of steaming rice the words "new age," "Messiah" and "last days of the old world" kept turning in my thoughts. The veil of mystery was lifting. I had won a glimpse of something that seemed to explain the Family's sacrificial spirit and their apparent harmony and joy.

Then Daniel shot into the room and whisked up beside me. "Well, what do you think?" Daniel's eyes gazed wide and earnest.

"A fantastic workshop, some amazing concepts," I began. Then I realized he was wondering if I wanted to join. "And I think you're the most amazing bunch of people I've ever met" (which I meant). "And I know I'll probably move in sooner or later, maybe in a year or so." I hoped it sounded convincing.

His eyes flashed disappointment; then he smiled and shrugged, "Why don't you come to the history lectures tomorrow night?" After a moment of hesitation I told him I would.

I suddenly realized how naive I'd been these past two weeks. Although I *was* aware that the Family welcomed, even encouraged those who wanted to join to do so, I'd been under the impression that the Family was also dedicated to sharing its ideals, hopes and philosophies simply to benefit people *outside* the group. Now it hit me like a pie in the face that the Family's primary and sole objective was to recruit members.

Yet for me it was the same old story. As deeply impressed as I was with the Family, I just didn't want to "join" or "move in." I had great plans, *wonderful* plans for my life. Committing myself to such an intense group effort as the Family would only hamstring my life strategies.

I had such great plans, such incredible hope for my life that sometimes my chest would swell hot with joy and hope. Man, there was so much to learn, to see, to touch, to experience! I literally wanted to do *everything*—sail around the world, write a novel, sky-dive, read the great philosophers and statesmen, mingle with the great minds of the university, get into peer counseling and community projects, explore Spain through Berkeley's Junior Year Abroad program.

It was almost uncanny, this youthful ambition, this *joie de vivre.* These last two years had been the most exciting and happiest years of my life. It was as if I'd wakened from a dream at age 16 and found myself standing on an enchanted forest path. And since then life had careened through endless adventure and fascination that I hoped would never end. Such indomitable hope, such dreams and such joy swelled in and consumed this young man's soul.

Though I didn't want to join the Family, the group did hold a place in my scheme of lofty life strategies. I believed that the Family would enable me to acquire *tools*, tools which would help me to love and serve with kindness, help me to live with more energy, help me to accomplish my goals.

But it seemed clear that a live-in commitment to the group and my personal life drama were incompatible. Although the Family was definitely a *part* of my youthful odyssey, a *part* of my life, I didn't want it to *be* my life.

Peter and I didn't like Isaiah Reez's history lecture Monday night, especially the elaboration on the numerology which "proved" when the Messiah would come again.

"Sounds like a bunch of juggled numbers to me," said Peter.

"Yup, my thoughts exactly. And I'd sure like to know who they think the Messiah is. Do you suppose they think it's Onni?"

Peter's hawkish eyes scanned the lecture room as it slowly emptied out. "Dunno. Lynn mentioned this Sun Myung Moon guy who founded the Family. I saw his picture when I was looking for Lynn on the second floor at Dana Street."

"Let's go," I said.

We met Daniel at the bottom of the stairs, and our suspicion and hostility blew up in his face like a short-fused cherry bomb.

"And who do you think the Messiah is?" asked Peter.

He shrunk back with a cornered-dog grimace.

"Well I have my own opinion and I . . ."

"Oh come off it, Daniel," I said. "Is it that Korean guy Sun Myung Moon?"

Daniel hesitated. "Well yes, that's right. But—"

After a few more minutes of confrontation Daniel encouraged us to hear out the second half of the history lectures. Then I started heading for the door. "I don't know, Daniel, . . . I have a lot of things to think over now."

After that uncomfortable incident I decided to take a breather and stay away from the center. I'd been visiting the Community almost every day for two solid weeks which, due to the intense workshops, seemed more like two months.

When I finished my homework Tuesday night I dragged a chair onto the balcony of my overflow room and watched the night parachute onto the city. I began to contemplate the strange design which life seemed to be weaving around me. Things were happening much too quickly. For 18 years I'd lived with my folks and now I wanted to strike out on my own, live alone, run my own life independent of outside interference.

Now after two weeks it struck me that my striving for independence, for personal sovereignty, was being threatened. Arlane and Daniel wanted to make a member out of me. And to complicate matters, something else had popped into the scenario—this Messiah business which I didn't know *what* to make of.

Two days later Peter and I were squeezing through the glass doors of the dorm lobby when my resident advisor, Laurie, motioned me to the desk. "Steve, some girl's been trying to call you for the past two days. Arlane or something . . ."

When I walked into my room I found a note on my desk.

Dear Steve,
How are you? We think about you all the time.
We all love you and heavenly Father loves you.
Love,
Arlane

What a corny note! But I had to laugh and was even touched that my Family-friend, Arlane, was thinking about me.

Peter and I then plopped down in turquoise vinyl lounge chairs with two cans of Mountain Dew and launched into our mutual pastime—analyzing the Family.

"I have to admire the way they center their lives on God," said Peter, "though I'm not very religious. My family's Lutheran and I stopped going to church in junior high. Still, I think about God once in a while and like to think that He is there."

"Yeah, I know what you mean. The Family treats God like an actual person, a Father who is right there with them. I like that. I was raised a Catholic and grew up perceiving God as some untouchable being who lived in the next galaxy."

We heard a knock and looked up to see a dimpled, grinning Arlane framed in the doorway. She chirped a greeting and swept into the room like a schoolgirl with a secret. We all laughed, then Peter blurted, "Cheez, Arlane, if I didn't know you were 28 I'd think you were 14!"

After we poked a little more fun at Arlane, she dropped the invitation, "Well, I was wondering if you guys would like to come over for dinner tonight."

Peter and I clammed up and scanned each other for a long three seconds. Then I shrugged; then Peter shrugged. "Sure. Why not? I'll get my car and you two wait for me on High Street," Peter agreed.

When I walked into Dana Street I met a barrage of joyful backslapping, hey-long-time-no-see whooping and Brothers and Sisters shaking my hands off. Then Lynn greeted Peter and he lit up like a store window at sunset.

Around nine o'clock Daniel and I went outside to talk in the cool night air. I think these conversations with Daniel and *Daniel himself* inspired me more than any other one thing about the Family. We'd become close since we'd met on Sproul Plaza that first day. And now I looked up to him like an older brother, a man of unselfish love, strength and seemingly boundless life-energy.

Monday night's confrontation and the issue of Sun Myung Moon's messiahship faded into obscurity and insignificance as he spoke about developing personal strengths, character and one's ability to love. Daniel leaned against the garden's rock wall, his tie hanging in a comfortable noose, the firm lines of his jaw silhouetted in the dim light of the street lamp.

"You know, Steve, people have no conception of their actual human potential. Man has *never* developed the full use of his faculties, *never* realized his natural state. Scientific evidence even demonstrates that on the whole, men employ only five percent of their brain's total working capacity."

Daniel then turned so I could see the coal specks of his eyes. "It's amazing. We were meant, in the very strictest sense, to become the *Sons* of *God*. You have to have a vision, Steve—a vision of your incredible potential." And inevitably, these inspirations kindled bonfires of personal hope and ambition and sent me spinning for hours in fantastic dreamworlds.

I suppose I admired Daniel and other older members because they seemed to practice what they preached. Daniel would stay up all night sometimes, counseling members with personal problems. He encouraged and supported; and when individuals were down he comforted them with kindness and understanding. Daniel's example started me thinking that if the Family had enabled him to become the impressive guy he was, then maybe the Family could help me grow in that way too.

There were three Berkeley juniors who'd recently joined the group. One of them was a remarkable 25-year-old named Fred Seymour. After a three-year Navy stint he'd enrolled in a junior college; and during his second year he was elected student body president of California's prestigious junior college system.

As the month of October frittered by, I grew to respect and like Fred as a man after my own heart. That a person of such experience, competence and character should join the Family gave me confidence that the group was in fact a good and legitimate organization.

October, 1973

Dear Mom and Dad,
How's the Indian October coming along? . . . Life is great here and the weather's still fantastic. Most of my courses are superbly interesting. For Biology 2 we're studying animal communities, our prof is really into termites. Afro-American studies is great because of the teacher. He's articulate, inspiring and black, and wears a Nairobi beany everyday.
Most of the people in the dorm are really nice. . . . We're all getting to know each other better. . . . Last night this guy who mountain-climbs climbed down from the seventh floor—as a publicity stunt for a party last night! At night everybody sits out on the balconies and watches the view of the Bay Area, and it's beautiful. So long, family.

Peace and love,
Steve

I devoted most of that weekend to enjoying myself with dorm buddies—chancing parties, bars and music spots; a nice change from the steamroller-workshops. Though I'd frequented Dana Street a lot since coming to Berkeley, during school days, on free evenings and after evenings at the center I'd spent time with my sixth-floor dorm crowd and with three college friends I really liked. Sean, from L.A., had roomed with me before the dorms opened up; Nester was a black student from San Jose who lived next door; Sandy was a wonderful freshman woman from the Mohave Desert in Southern California.

At Saturday night's floor party I worked the sound system with crazy joke-reeling Nester, and taught Sandy the jitterbug which I'd learned in France. Later Sandy and I hit a Turkish bar/restaurant which boasted a huge, scintillating neon message—"Our cooks eat here." Over beer and then Turkish espresso we philosophized into the tidbit hours. I did a lot of bar-philosophizing those first weeks in college. I loved it, and these times with Sandy and my other friends blossomed into precious memories in the years to come.

By Monday afternoon I'd been away from the center for three days, the longest time ever. And I felt caught in the middle of a tug-of-war between two realities: the academic-college reality, and the Family's "spiritual reality." One hour I'd think the Family was the only bunch of people who had it together. The next hour I'd realized that many of the viewpoints and life-styles of professors and students were just as valid and sensible, if not more so.

By Monday evening this buffeting between my two realities drove me to scrawl out a list of questions about Family doctrine and practices and then hitchhike to Dana Street to pose them to Daniel. This hadn't been the first time I'd assaulted him with lists of questions. In fact my constant questioning at workshops and evening programs had won me a reputation as an ardent questioner. I'd probably inherited this characteristic from my scientist-Dad who took almost everything with a grain of salt.

As usual, Daniel responded with *some* answers, a good deal of vagueness and an occasional, "I'm not sure, I'll have to ask Onni." He used the latter response with my following question—"I'm still wondering what happened to Jesus' body if He wasn't physically resurrected?" Daniel was "almost positive" that the disciples had stolen the body.

Some Family beliefs I found completely erroneous, for instance their belief that individuals fall asleep in Divine Principle lectures because they come under attack from evil "sleep spirits" determined to block earthlings from hearing "the truth." They fell asleep because they were exhausted. Yet in the final analysis, my brain-wracking always returned to the same compelling thought—"How can a group of such wonderful intelligent people all be wrong and I right?"

The next day as I was picking my way through dense rivers of students, I suddenly saw the Berkeley crowd as so many depressed soulless bodies wandering through life without purpose, hope or direction. I had slipped into this point of view several times that week, but never so acutely.

I recalled Joshua's testimony at the last workshop: "Everyone's out to take from each other in this world. That's why there's no true love in the world." And Dr. Durst's moving discourses on our planet's greed and malice spun in my thoughts like a blackjack wheel. I began thinking that maybe the Family was right, maybe the world *was* sick and dying; maybe there *was* no true love outside the Family.

Wednesday evening I tucked myself away in my favorite study spot—a quiet corner on the fifth floor of the undergraduate library. All night I tried studying my calculus, but just couldn't concentrate. Like numbers flashing at the outset of a film reel, the same images turned in my thoughts—smiling faces of Family members, workshop lectures, the youthful portrait of Sun Myung Moon on the inside cover of the *Divine Principle* book.

In the last few days it had dawned on me that the Family was making claims I could no longer ignore or regard only as interesting philosophies. I also realized it would become increasingly difficult to continue courting this religious community as simply a stimulating after-school hobby. The possum was out of the bag—Family members were claiming to be followers of the *Lord of the Second Advent* (Christ returned).

Over and over, the same thoughts pestered me like a cloud of pursuing mosquitoes, "Is this thing true or isn't it true—this revelation of divine principles, this man Sun Myung Moon?"

I eventually slapped the textbook shut and began leafing through the spiral notebooks I'd crammed with workshop lecture notes. Throughout, red-inked question marks flashed like stoplights, labeling ideological questions and skeptical comments. Though I was both skeptical and impressed with the Divine Principle, now certain tenets seemed to make a lot of sense. For instance, the Family believed that spiritual laws govern the spiritual universe just as the laws of science govern the physical universe. I thought, *Doesn't it seem logical that God would want us to understand the nature of our spiritual universe just as we are coming to understand our physical universe?* Wouldn't the Creator eventually want to reveal to His children the truth about how and why they were created, how they fell into sin, why a history of suffering has dragged on for thousands of years? Why couldn't man have *answers* to these very basic questions? Not answers in terms of vague religious doctrines which required huge amounts of faith, but answers on par with scientific law?

And I'd never had any trouble sympathizing with the Family's belief that God intended for man to live in a perfect, sinless world; a global family where God and God's love was everyone's electric and power company. I found the Family's logic very compelling here. As Isaiah Reez once put it: "And what's really so absurd about an ideal world? Isn't it far more absurd that God would want to perpetuate a world where His children are starved, oppressed and murdered?"

After aeons of staring at the plaster walls I became aware of a hounding sense of urgency to get to the bottom of this mystery called "the Family." Something Daniel had said at the close of the workshop rang in my thoughts—"I know it's fantastic, the idea that we are living during the time in history when the Messiah comes to complete God's providence; but even if there's only *one chance* in a *million* that this is true, don't you think you owe it to yourself to find out for sure?"

In addition there was a sense of urgency which the Family's *ideology* demanded. It taught that all of God's central figures, even Jesus, had failed God; and now He was counting on US (on *me*!) to comfort His heart and work for the realization of the ideal world.

I didn't sleep well that night and woke Thursday morning to find my brain humming a popular tune "Today" adopted by the Family. The bard sang of how a million tomorrows would pass him by if he ever forgot the joy that was his that day.

Now the feeling of urgency had expanded into a trembling sensation that I was standing on the threshold of losing something very precious. If I took this joy for granted, this *joie de vivre* I'd experienced during my weeks of communing with this superbly idealistic family, and remained a distant observer, would a million tomorrows of happiness eventually slip through my fingers? Suppose I got lazy and didn't try to find out what this group was about; might I eventually lose interest and drift away, and pass up precious wisdom and understanding, a million tomorrows of growing and developing in heart and spirit in a most wonderful way?

After my calculus class I slipped into the library and climbed to my fifth-floor perch. I was determined to knock off my physics homework. Instead I spent the entire day staring at printed pages and sterile walls, agonizing about the Family. If I fought to concentrate, only a few minutes passed before the same thoughts came flurrying back: *Is it true or isn't it true? Who is this man Sun Myung Moon?* I realized that if I ignored the movement and it turned out to be what it claimed to be, then I would be turning my back on the truth, on God Himself. I'd be denying ideals I'd come to cherish, denying great hopes of alleviating some of the suffering in the world.

By midafternoon the dissonance was shrieking inside my head like a horde of bats. I felt I was under attack, and that this was what it was like to lose one's mind, to slip into the deep end. Finally, I knew I *had* to come to a decision—I would move in Friday night.

I *had* to crack this mystery. Trying the Family out for a few weeks or months seemed my only recourse. By becoming a part of this Community, and living as they lived, I hoped to solve the mystery surrounding the claims of the Unification Church.

I did *not* come to this decision as a commitment to following the Divine Principle or Sun Myung Moon, neither of which I thought merited my trust or acceptance. Rather, I decided to "move in" in order to learn about the group firsthand. In other words, my decision was by no means a handing over of my life, . . . it was an *experiment.*

In the end I overcame my fear of losing my freedom and independence to the group. I reasoned that as a student I could lead a separate life on campus and so maintain a large degree of independence.

One thought gave me confidence that my decision was an absolutely safe one—*If in time I get sick and tired of this way of life, or it becomes clear that it's false, I can always leave.*

There were at least a dozen factors that brought about my "joining" the group. But I did manage to wrestle out two clearcut conscious reasons for my actions. The first reason stemmed from a desire to know God in the deeply personal way Family members seemed to know Him.

The second and by far the more important reason was related to the seemingly great potential for personal growth in the Family. The desire to develop my potential, to become a

more giving, more loving person flowed in me deep and strong.
And this Community seemed an ideal environment for learning
and growing in this way since everyone lived for similar ideals
and supported each other.

Nearly four weeks of part-time but intensive group involvement had lapsed since I first met Arlane on Sproul Plaza. By
this time I looked upon certain Family members as some of the
most amazing and wonderful people I'd ever known. In the
brilliant light of this courageous band of new-age pioneers,
anyone I'd ever loved and respected faded into obscurity and
insignificance—even my mom whom I loved more than anyone
or anything in the world; even my dad who I believed was one of
the world's most brilliant men; even that dear Jesuit, Father
McDonald; even my lifelong buddy Jim Britt.

Perhaps this was due to the supernatural aura which enveloped the group, its promises of a better world, its constant
reference to God and the spiritual world on the other side of
death. Now, friends, family, Mom and Dad seemed much more
than thousands of miles away. They seemed decades away—
grey memories; blurred and faded ghosts of the past.

Though my moving into the center on Dana Street was an
experiment, it was an experiment I took seriously. And by this
time I'd learned that Family members didn't date. Conclusion:
if I was truly going to live the way they lived, it meant that my
heavy dating days were over.

At first this "no-dating" group standard had really bothered
me; I'd always been hopelessly girl-crazy. But the Family had
fostered in me a growing awareness of life after death, of the
spiritual universe and of death itself; accordingly, girl
thoughts and sexual thoughts fled my consciousness and slipped into the dark, oozing bog of insignificance which had
already swallowed up the memory of family and friends.
Perhaps some time in the future I would "go out" on occasion;
but the present situation seemed to compel that I say good-bye
to Sandy and take her out one last time.

Somewhere around 2:00 A.M. Sandy and I were standing
outside a bar on Telegraph holding each other. I'd just spilled
the news about moving in with "the people on Dana Street."
When she asked me why I couldn't stay in the dorm I knew I was
going to miss her. Suspended in the fresh night air, I hugged

Sandy as if it were the last time I'd ever hug a woman. And I realized I was giving up something very precious by throwing in my lot with this group. Was I nuts? Was it worth it? But somehow I believed that I would gain so much more in return. So much more. That was my hope.

October, 1973
Dear Jim Babes [Jim Britt],
. . . I'm moving in with this big "family" of 80 people. This may sound funny, but my whole life stands at a turning point because of this decision. . . . It's not really a commune but there is a set of principles which holds the Family together. I'm not joining because of the principles but because the people in the Family are the nicest, far-outest, most open and loving people I have ever met in my life.

What makes this family . . . so amazing is that they practice what they preach! . . . They live life to *give* of themselves. . . . And I want to learn the secret of what makes them so happy; because Family members are (and I'm not kidding you, Jim) the happiest people I've ever met. They just glow, just being with them makes me feel happy and warm inside. This may sound kind of corny, but I think the secret is love. I want to learn how to truly and unselfishly love. This doesn't make much sense so I'll write later!

On a drizzling Friday night in late October, 1973 I threw my belongings in a green dufflebag, checked out of the dorm, and tramped the 10-block pilgrimage to the center. When I strolled in, dripping and triumphant, the Brothers and Sisters screamed for joy! Steve Kemperman had joined the Family, had begun a new life, had passed into the realms of another world.

Chapter Eight

Indoctrination

*"You have been liberated now.
We shall not harm you. No . . .
we shall deliberately preserve your
lives and help you to learn the truth,"*
Commandant,
POW camp in Korea, 1954. [6]

It was 1:15 A.M. when I returned from a long Sunday night at the library. I strode through Regent Street's front door into the coal blackness of the living room and sank a Frye boot into a soft, heavy bundle. Muffled groan. When my eyes accustomed to the darkness I saw an ocean of wall-to-wall sleeping bags stretching across the living and dining rooms—giant cocoons with protruding white faces. The last of the Brothers were bedding down in a far corner.

My sleeping bag draped over an arm, I entered the study and jammed the door against something. Thinking it was a chair I tried to heave it aside. Muffled groan. I flicked the light on. I'd vigorously wedged the door into Jim Arle's side!

The room looked like a jar of stuffed olives. Daniel slept half underneath the bureau. Guy Fenner had propped the feet-end of his sleeping bag on Stefan. Others lay jigsawed over every patch of floor space. I had to chuckle. Absurd living conditions, but I had to admire their spirit of sacrifice.

On the other hand, the Brothers' faces didn't look peaceful; rather they were etched with lines of fatigue, strangely old. Even their eyes were sunken and underlined with bags of dark, puffy skin. When Jim didn't wake up for an apology I cut the light and closed the door.

I could have sworn I'd *just* laid my weary body on the living room floor when the ceiling lights switched on and a Brother began stomping around the room. "Rise and shine, Family! It's time for a brand new day!" I squinted at my watch. Yuk, 5:45 A.M. Suddenly Luke, who was lying next to me, yelled, "OK, trinity. Let's *jump it*!" Four sleeping bags rocketed to a standing position and peeled to the floor like cocoons ejecting butterflies. Then the Brothers fluttered off to the bathroom.

I considered giving somebody a brand new day right in the nose. We couldn't have slept much more than four-and-a-half hours! I felt limp and nailed to the floor, a shipwrecked sailor washed up on the beach. I was in no shape to tackle the day ahead, at least not with my usual energy and clarity of mind.

After some prodding by Joshua's nail-on-blackboard exhortations, I dragged my body to its feet. With 40 Brothers in the house, the bathroom squirmed like a bowl of jellyfish. Bare feet splatted. The sink and shower ran nonstop above the rumble of laughter and conversation. "Come on, Abraham! You've been in there over two minutes now." Then Daniel bellowed, "One-minute showers! Only one-minute showers. We're going to time you!" Then he laughed to soften the command.

Minutes later the Sisters came downstairs and everyone lined up in the living room for morning exercises. Then during an impressive 15-minute cleanup period members scrambled like beavers, stacking sleeping bags and vacuuming floors.

By 6:25 A.M. the entire Family sat scrunched around the coffee table at Dana Street for a combination morning gathering and worship service. Luke sat on his haunches at the head of the table, and he and Christine led us in song.

I couldn't help but notice the changed atmosphere—so different from that of the workshops and evening programs. Maybe the members were early-morning groggy, but I almost didn't recognize where I was. The songs sounded grinding and mechanical, as if the members were trying to whip up their spirits rather than worship or give thanks to God.

Then Luke conjured up some stapled pages of print. "Let's open our hearts now as we read 'Master Speaks.' " Although I'd never heard of these writings, it didn't take long to figure out that they were Sun Myung Moon's speeches to the worldwide Family.

This was followed with the pleas and whines of 80 members praying in unison. "Oh *yes*, heavenly Father! Oh pleeeeeeeez, heavenly Father!"

During the announcements Luke punched the air and called us to action. "Hey, Family! Let's bring those heavenly children to the weekend workshop. Everyone should have a guest by Friday. Father is counting on you!" And that morning I learned that our "Father" was Sun Myung Moon.

Then we broke up into "trinities" to study the "Master Speaks" and eat cold pancakes, syrup and orange juice. Of course I ended up in Daniel's trinity and he springboarded us into the day with a bang of inspiration. Playfully shoulder-punching me, he said, "Be an example of a man alive! Have a great day and love no matter what!"

At 7:30 Daniel shot off to work in San Francisco, Fred Seymour and I to our classes, and the others to the flower-selling teams, maintenance company or garden company.

During those first weeks in the Unification Church I met a barrage of beliefs, practices and rituals which I hadn't known before I'd moved in. It was like a train ride through a fairground spook-house—almost every day some odd belief or ritual would pop out in front of me like a skeleton swinging out from the darkness, or a half-decomposed body sitting up in a casket.

I'll never forget my first "Pledge Service," which takes place at 5:00 A.M. the first Sunday of each month throughout the worldwide Family. Family members stood lined up, slicked and prim, in front of a coffee table bearing two burning candles and a portrait of Mr. and Mrs. Moon.

"Now let us bow to our True Parents!" said Christine. Suddenly everyone crossed hands at the forehead and bowed to a fetal kneeling position. I stood paralyzed with horror and revulsion. I'd been tricked; they hadn't told me about *this*! After the second bow Christine pinned me with vehement witch-eyes; a moment later I was prostrated before the "True Parents."

Gripping "pledge cards" we then recited "My Pledge" in blasting unison: "As a true son (or daughter), I will follow our Father's pattern and charge bravely forward into the enemy camp until I have judged them completely with the weapons with which He has been defeating the enemy Satan . . ." After about two minutes of pledging we exploded into a kamikaze-like vow: "I will fight with my life! I will be responsible for accomplishing my duty and mission. This I pledge and swear! This I pledge and swear! This I pledge and swear!"[7]

That week was *full* of surprises! Isaiah told me Korean would be the language of the ideal world, and Lisa explained what "holy salt" was—table salt blessed by "Father" and used to purify physical things of the fallen world like groceries, clothes and gifts. Whether flabbergasted or hostilely skeptical about these bolts out of the blue, I usually told myself, *OK don't get excited. You decided to try out the Family; so at least give it a chance and stick around for a while.*

It was late Sunday night when a Sister started yelping, "Onni's here! Onni's here!" Then Onni and Christine (her right-hand person) swept into Dana Street and claimed a couch. In the rush to gather around, staff members scurried to kneel at Onni's feet and fix her with worshiping gazes.

"Thank you for being part of Family," she began in her thick Korean accent. "We are first people to truly actualize the truth. We are first people to walk this path in history. It's a very difficult path. Therefore, you have to relate to Principle, mature with Principle . . ."[8]

At first the beautiful Onni radiated warm, motherly affection. Later she spoke sternly: "You have many concepts, many philosophies from your experiences. But we must be children with open hearts and learn again. If you have concepts, put them away! . . ."[9] I realized the staff used this same argument on young members (like me) who had reservations about a Family practice or belief—"Come on now, NO CONCEPTS!"

Suddenly Onni extended an arm and pointed in my direction. "YOU! You, and you! Stand up! All new members to your feet!" We moved. "Do you agree that we must establish ideal person and ideal world? And do you want to work with us? And do you promise to do very best?"

"Yes."

"What?! I can't hear you!"

"Yes!"

"Sit down."

My life-style changed radically the moment I entered the Family's world. I slept four-and-a-half to five hours a night, studied and ate only with student members or with Blossom at the Sproul Plaza table. And I never saw my dorm buddies anymore. Another person I never saw again was Peter Norchrist. He dropped out of the Family scene when his fiancée came in from Massachusetts. Peter probably felt that he had too much to lose by committing himself to the Family; namely his future wife and the establishment of that cozy family niche he had so often talked about.

Fred Seymour on the other hand became a precious study companion, a warm and terrifically humorous guy. We kept each other awake; and when the drowziness seemed unbeatable we ran circles around the library. Some of the battles with sleep bordered on the beautifully ludicrous. During one of Jacob and Fred's comparative religion classes they both stood in the back "to fight it out." With their noses pointed to the ceiling and their mouths agape, they snored like rhinos.

I struggled with concepts. *Are the things they're teaching me really true? Such as the idea that Buddhist spirits direct Buddhists to the Principle! Or that much mental illness is caused by being possessed by evil spirits? It seems all so crazy.*

At morning trinity meetings I presented Daniel with lists of questions about Divine Principle and Family practices. One aspect of the group which infuriated me was the constant harping on evil spirits: a member fell asleep because a "sleep spirit" forced his eyes closed (student members included); if he was swamped with sexual desires, it was the onslaught of "lust spirits"; and around each member battled a myriad of good and evil spirits, all vying to work through him, either for or against "the Restoration."

Members constantly fought to "knock out negativity." During a weekend restaurant job with the maintenance company, I noticed that Joshua and Jim Arle were falling asleep over their carpet shampooers. Suddenly they began chanting, "Out *Satan!* Out *Satan!* Out *Satan!*"

These beliefs seemed so irrational (especially the "sleep spirit" beliefs since members obviously didn't get enough sleep) that I debated them fiercely with student members, and wrote up counter arguments. When I presented these essays to Daniel he only chuckled in admiration and told our trinity, "I wish all of you wanted to learn and understand as much as Stevie here." I never did get any real answers from Daniel, mostly evasions and compliments.

Now don't get me wrong. There were also *good* days when being in the Family brought me special joy. My diary entry for November, 1973 said, "Wow, what a powerful day! I finished the scratch copy on my critical film essay and went home to eat and drink hot chocolate and rap on the deepest subjects. . . . The place was packed! And what spirit. People's faces were shining all night.

"Our trinity meeting was flying ten feet off the ground. [Daniel] told us about his day—greatest day of his life . . ."

> Dear Dadio, (referring to God)
> . . . This morning we went to the Holy Grounds again. The circle of grass frontiered by the twelve trees was unspeakably pure. The dew, sparkling drops of wetness. The sun on the grass. The shimmering waters of Lake Merrit. . . . And holding the hands of my beautiful Brothers and Sisters, I just knew that it all came from you, that you really do have the greatest of hearts.

(When Sun Myung Moon first came to the U.S. in 1965 he blessed 120 plots of land throughout America, mostly in public parks, and designated them "Holy Grounds.")

Another surprise package was the Family's absolute standard on short hair. I had sincerely thought the Family would at least tolerate my nearly shoulder-length hair. But after three-and-a-half weeks of bucking their hair rules, I felt the staff people starting to come down hard.

"It's against the purpose of the whole," said Daniel as our trinity drove back from an ice cream jaunt. "And in any case, you have to follow 'center-man.' " I finally got a haircut to make everybody happy and get them off my back.

In a trinity meeting shortly afterwards, Guy Fenner, a three-month member, and I learned that "Father" would someday choose our spouses: Messiah or not, we both thought this sounded mighty scary. My prayer in my diary was "Help me

God. Yes I am thankful for being in this Family, but only as a learning experience. Help me to know whether they live the highest truth possible, whether this is it, whether this is the last Messiah."

On the last night of the Thanksgiving workshop at Booneville I was overcome by negativity. Perhaps it was the "Master Speaks" on the marriage ceremonies or the numerology which seemed so arbitrary. I couldn't dig it.

One late November morning as I walked to school, thoughts of moving back into the dorm or into my own apartment whirled like night bats. I'd recently been hit by a wave of disillusionment about the whole experience of living in the Family.

Was I simply a pawn in some huge mass movement? Sometimes I felt so manipulated. Unless you were a leader there was no real, creative, responsibility-taking work. The most disillusioning experience of all was that the love and attention I had come to know before moving had *vanished*. It had turned out that this love phenomenon was nothing more than "love bombing"—a show of great affection and concern for guests which would hopefully influence them to stay with the Family.

It began to drizzle. Then I remembered something Christine had mentioned at a late-night Family meeting. "When you first join the Family you enjoy a kind of honeymoon period. Heavenly Father protects you with His love so you'll grow quickly and learn about the Family. But after about a month heavenly Father withdraws His protection in order to let Satan get a crack at you. God wants you to endure this trial so that you'll become strong." I slowed down to a crawl. *Oh my God. I've been in the Family just over a month!* Then I thought the inevitable: *Could my honeymoon period be over? . . . Could these thoughts of moving out of the Family be from Satan?!* In the end, afraid that I was enduring some kind of spiritual test, I took no action whatsoever.

During my first months in the Oakland-Berkeley center I heard several stories about the gruesome fate of members who left the Family. During a Sunday night dinner, Rhonda told me about a Sister who'd recently left. "I went to visit a few times to try to get her to come back. . . . Her face was pale and haggard and she stared real crazy-like with this empty, defeated look. I finally gave up. She was *dead*, spiritually *dead!*"

There were also tales of satanic possession and of ex-members being struck and killed by cars. Another Sister told me how she'd left the group after a month and moved into an apartment in Berkeley. For weeks she lived with constant confusion, fear and guilt. She kept thinking about how she was failing God, the entire spirit world, and all her ancestors (who could only be restored to perfection through "*you*," a follower of the Messiah). She couldn't shake thoughts of how she lived only for herself while Family members sacrificed everything for God and all mankind. After six weeks she returned.

Though some issues provoked doubts about the group, others inspired acceptance of the Family as Messiah's movement. One December morning, Isaiah was moderating the meeting and he bowled us over with chillingly fantastic predictions of success within the coming three years: "People will be waiting in line to join! We'll have to rent huge auditoriums for mass workshops!"

Then one December evening when Daniel and I were camped on the yellow shag rug, I mentioned my plans to enroll in the Junior Year Abroad program to study at the University of Madrid. "Why in two years you'll be a world leader!" said Daniel, eyes aglow with visionary light.

I didn't know exactly what he meant by "world leader," but I was certainly flattered that he thought me capable of such a feat. I did know however of Father's proclamations that in the course of world restoration, Unification Church members would become the leaders of entire nations.

> December 15, 1973 (Last entry in my Oakland-Berkeley diary)
> . . . It's been almost three weeks since I've heard a Principle lecture series. So today, all the lectures really hit me anew, and they make so much more sense now.

Final exams and the Christmas holidays rolled around. Two months had passed since I'd moved into the Family. Though I still considered my schoolwork more important than center activities, I did dedicate most weekends to working with the maintenance company or the flower-selling teams. I had entered the movement thinking, *Is the Divine Principle true? Well, I'm going to question and investigate it to find out if it's true.* By mid-December my thinking had changed.

In late November Joshua and other staff members confronted me with a new line of reasoning. They said, "All this studying and questioning is OK, but the best way to understand the Divine Principle is to *live it.* Apply the Divine Principle to your life, *practice* it, giving yourself fully to your Family mission, to serving the cause. Then you'll find out if the Divine Principle works. And if it *works*, then it must be *true*."

I guess at some point I became so frustrated in my struggles to fathom certain Divine Principle concepts which seemed flaky or illogical that I began experimenting with the above line of reasoning. This strategy of "find out whether it's true by finding out whether it works" circumvented an intellectual approach to examining the Divine Principle and cast a mystical aura over the ideology and my entire Family experience. One of the by-products of this line of reasoning was the notion that in order to uncover the truth about the Divine Principle and the group, one had to develop a certain spiritual insight. The mind by itself could not fathom this vast teaching.

Experimenting with this "spiritual approach" in examining the Family, plus the countless lectures, and arguments and talks with leaders, finally broke my skepticism and doubt. On top of that, I was tired of playing the part of the analytical, intellectual skeptic, the doubting Thomas.

By the end of December I had begun to think and view the world as all members did. I'd even begun talking about evil spirits as everyone else talked about them. In fact these denizens of the netherworld became as real for me as the whirring, blood-glutted mosquitoes of hot summer nights.

My attitude towards the ideology was now, "The *Divine Principle is true*. You don't question the truth, you *learn it*." And from that point on, overlooking very occasional doubts, I unquestioningly accepted the policies and teachings of Father and the leadership as God's absolute truth.

The Family's reality became my reality. At last I knew that it was true. I, Steve Kemperman, was a pioneer disciple of God's living Messiah. And together we would build the perfect world of the last days.

Chapter Nine

The Messiah!

"The Day of hope is coming to end the long dark night. The people of earth discerning the one of truth and light. From the East he's coming, a beaming, glorious sight. O day of hope! O day of light! O day of history."[10]

The 21-city Day of Hope Tour was Father's second campaign to bring America to the True Parents. After our leader spoke in Carnegie Hall, New York on October 1, 1973 he began crisscrossing westward through America and by the last week in January would reach the twenty-first and last city, Los Angeles, California. (The first Day of Hope Tour in 1971-72 blitzed seven American and three European cities.)

Sun Myung Moon spoke three nights in each city on three respective themes: "God's Hope for Man," "God's Hope for America," and "The Future of Christianity." On the evening of the opening day of each talk-series, local VIPs were treated to a posh banquet and a speech by "The Reverend Sun Myung Moon." In preparation for these Day of Hope banquets we sent out hundreds of invitations and visited prominent church leaders, businessmen and politicians.

We in Berkeley were moved and awed that the Messiah was now sweeping through the country towards California, preaching the kingdom of heaven was at hand, as Jesus had 2,000 years ago. Though Jesus had been unsuccessful in establishing the heavenly kingdom, we were confident that with a lot of hard work, sacrifice and faith, the second Christ would not fail this time around.

Who is this man Sun Myung Moon? What puzzle of events led him into his messianic mission and to where he is today? Much of what I learned about Father I read in "Master Speaks" and other Family publications. A portion was gleaned from a fascinating oral tradition passed down from the leadership.

Sun Myung Moon was born January 6, 1920 in the village of Kwangju Sangsa Ri in the Pyungan Bukedo province in north-western Korea. I was told that January sixth was the actual date of Jesus' birth. Our leader's original name was *Yong* Myung Moon, which for many people means "Shining Dragon." In the mid-1940s he changed his name to *Sun* Myung Moon. He is the second son in a farmer's family of two boys and six girls. When he was 10 his family converted to Christianity and joined the Presbyterian church.

The young Korean was known as an audacious and extremely ambitious young lad. He resolved to become a great scholar and earn three Ph.D.s. At 15, Father became poignantly aware of the world's suffering and ultimately decided he would not rest until he had liberated the entire human race from its misery and hurt.

On Easter morning in 1936, Sun Myung Moon was deep in prayer on a Korean mountainside when Jesus Christ appeared to him and asked him to complete the mission of world restoration which Jesus had been unable to accomplish. At first the 16-year-old hesitated because he knew that once he promised to take on this mission, before God and Jesus he could never turn back. Again and again, Jesus asked the chosen boy to accept, saying that he, Sun Myung Moon, was the only one who could fulfill the mission. After much agonizing the young Korean accepted the immense task of world salvation.

During the next nine years Sun Myung Moon prepared himself through intense study and prayer. In those years he began to discover the "divine principles." He read voraciously and carried a Bible wherever he went. He sought out and questioned spiritual leaders both in Korea and in the spirit world, e.g. Buddha, Confucius and Jesus.

Our leader realized he had to be able to understand and relate to all men in order to save them. So he determined to broaden his experiences. He gave free haircuts to the ghetto poor. Attempting to understand the rich he spent a night in the city's most luxurious hotel, eating rich food and bathing in milk.

Gradually, Father came to know the lonely and grieving heart of God who wept over the sinful state of the world. And though many women were attracted to Father, he always remained pure; one woman even wrote him a love letter with her own blood.

But most horrific of all were our leader's fierce battles in the spirit world with Satan and his legions of evil spirits who were determined to turn Sun Myung Moon away from his mission. Father once said, "If anyone knew what I passed through during those years, his heart would stop in shock and sorrow. No one is capable of bearing the story."[11]

During World War II Sun Myung Moon studied electrical engineering at Waseda University in Tokyo. In 1945 Korea was liberated from the Japanese and he began preaching the truths which had been revealed to him. This marked the beginning of Sun Myung Moon's public ministry.

During a six-month period in 1946 Father left his followers in Pyongyang, North Korea to live with a religious community north of Seoul called Israel Soodo Won (Israel Monastery). The group was headed by Paik Moon Kim, a man who openly proclaimed himself as Messiah. Father said he humbled himself to Kim and never admitted that he, Sun Myung Moon, was the true Messiah. (I never could figure out why Father stayed with Israel Monastery.*)

And at last, when Father knew he had completely uncovered God's "Divine Principle" he went before God and asked, "The Divine Principle is true, isn't it?" Twice God denied it and sent Father away to study more. The third time around God admitted that the Divine Principle was indeed the truth. At that point the entire spirit world bowed down to Sun Myung Moon.

By mid-1946 Sun Myung Moon had already gained a considerable following in Pyongyang and he came to the attention of the communist authorities. At the time they were ruthlessly persecuting Christian churches. One night in August, 1946 the communists dragged Father off to the Daedong police station where he was tortured and beaten terribly and finally left

---

* It is believed that Moon incorporated many concepts which he encountered at Israel Monastery into his own theology, the "*Divine Principle.*"

for dead on the garbage heap out back. His followers came for Sun Myung Moon's broken body to give it a Christian burial, but then discovered that miraculously he was still alive. He was then nurtured back to health.

Sun Myung Moon continued to preach as if nothing had happened. Then in 1948 the communists arrested him a second time and sentenced him to five years of hard labor at a concentration camp in Hung Nam. When he arrived at the labor camp he knew he had been sent there to die. Prisoners were deliberately overworked and underfed and usually survived no more than six months. For long hours they mined, packed and loaded heavy bags of lime, sometimes with bare hands.

Moon resolved to survive all hardships. If he died, the world would continue in suffering for centuries to come. He decided to surpass the unattainable work quotas, and not only surpassed them but received an award from his jailers for his outstanding work record. At night he prayed, comforting God's heart and assuring the heavenly Father that he would not be defeated by his suffering. And he did not become emaciated as did other prisoners.*

Though he could never speak about the Divine Principle, even in prison he won followers, men who had been inspired to seek him out by dreams and visions and by Father's example as a man of God.

In June 1959, the Korean War broke out. Soon thereafter, as United Nations forces advanced from the sea, prison authorities began executing prisoners. The day before it was Father's turn to be shot the UN forces began a naval gun bombardment at Hung Nam. The communists fled leaving the prisoners to be freed by UN troops October 14, 1950.

Carrying a broken-legged follower on his back, according to the Church, Sun Myung Moon bicycled 600 miles over refugee-clogged mountain trails to the South Korean city of Pusan. Here he began to preach the "Principles," working the cold docks as a harbor laborer at night.

In 1952 Mrs. Hyun-sil Kang became Sun Myung Moon's first woman follower. She was a student at a Christian semi-

---

* I have heard several accounts by church leaders that Sun Myung Moon received gifts such as shoes and food from his prisoner-followers.

nary and a church evangelist. She originally went to Father to witness to him. Instead she was attracted by his ideas. "One time Father told her to pray to ask God who is higher, Father or Jesus. . . . By that time she really felt this was not an ordinary teacher; she was afraid of him and she followed."[12]

In May, 1954 Sun Myung Moon officially established his church, the Tongil-Kyo, which in English means the Holy Spirit Association for the Unification of World Christianity.

The church endured many rocky years following its initiation. In 1954 our leader's wife of 10 years left him because she could not comprehend Father's mission and wanted him only for herself. Then in July, 1955 the Seoul police arrested Father and several chief followers. They spent three months in jail, and the original charges of draft dodging were later changed to "communal sex" and ultimately dropped.* Apparently, the Christian community believed Father practiced secret sexual rites amongst his members. In fact several professors and students were expelled from their universities for participating in the "scandalous rites of the Unification Church."[13]

In the course of a short decade Sun Myung Moon progressed from a spiritual leader living in a Pusan mud hut to a powerful and wealthy man leading thousands of followers and managing member-run factories which manufactured such varied products as air rifles, marble vases, tungsten and pharmaceutical supplies.

March, 1960 marked the date of the "Marriage Supper of the Lamb," the marriage of Sun Myung Moon and his 18-year-old bride, Hak Ja Han. Now that our leader has based his mission in America, the True Parents and their perfect children reside on a plush estate on the Hudson River near Tarrytown, New York.

Who is this man Sun Myung Moon? No matter how much I learned about him he always remained somewhat of a mystery. If anything about our Father amazed me or stood out in bold relief it was his incredible business savvy and his unwavering, almost ruthless, determination. The latter quality seemed to best encapsulate our leader's personality—once he set his mind on a goal, nothing, absolutely nothing would stop him from attaining it.

---

* When modest young Korean women refused to press charges because of family shame.

The Berkeley auditorium enjoyed a good turnout the first night of the Day of Hope talks. Following a worthy performance by the "New Hope Singers" and the Korean Folk Ballet, Neil Albert Salonen, president of the Unification Church of America, manned the lectern and delivered a short introduction. Then extending a heralding arm he half-shouted, "Ladies and gentlemen. May I present to you the Reverend Sun . . . Myung . . . Moon!"

Father's translator, Colonel Bo Hi Pak, looked lean and bony in contrast with Sun Myung Moon's stocky build, massive oval face and underscoring bull-jaw. It took Father only about 10 minutes to get warmed up. Soon his voice was rising to high pitched yelps and plunging to gutteral wheezing and growling. At times he gyrated his head, and the harsh, stacatto Korean would sound like an avalanche of rocks crashing on a kitchen floor.

The Colonel Pak began translating in his surprisingly refined English, Father would immediately pull back into a solemn dignified pose. A few minutes later Sun Myung Moon would be off and pounding the lectern, karate chopping the air, shaking his fist and then closing the delivery with impressive, well-coordinated antics.

One time he walked out from the lectern, spread his arms like a great condor and swung them together in an explosive clap. This was followed by a hands-on-hips gyration at the waist, a few stomps, and finally a beautifully executed ballet kick along with a half-hissed, half-growled Korean exclamation that sounded like "Sschaaaa!"

You couldn't overestimate the effect of this performance on the membership. We loved it and were captivated and mesmerized! Who else but the Messiah would have the guts to thunder truth the way this man did?

But not everyone was as impressed as we were. Dozens walked out with disgusted looks. And halfway through the talk a young guy wearing a Mexican smock leaned over the balcony railing and began shouting. The Korean duo fell silent. The young man said: "Hey lover boy! For the last hour I've been listening to you talk about love and the ideal. Why don't you talk some love into old Park Chung Hee? Like try doing something about the oppression and suffering in your *own* country before you go laying your love-trip on the whole world!" Suddenly two big security Brothers grasped the heckler's arms, pulled him back and scurried him up the aisle and out the door.

Very basically, Sun Myung Moon presented an evangelical-flavored summation of central "Divine Principle" themes: Principle of Creation, Fall of Man, Mission of Jesus. Naturally, he left out the heavy teachings so as not to turn anyone off.

On the third and last night Father discussed "The Future of Christianity." He proclaimed that Christianity is in a definite crisis, a crisis parallel to that of Jesus' time when the established religious institutions failed the Son of God: "It is the hope of Christianity to recognize, receive and accept the Lord of the Second Advent. . . . The greatest opportunity in any man's life is now knocking at our door. Please be humble, and open yourself to great new hope!"[14]

Colonel Pak translated. Then Father closed in a subdued, reverent voice: "There is opportunity . . . to come to our church and study, or attend our workshops and explore the truth of the Divine Principle. . . . I hope . . . you will consider these ideas seriously, and pray to God. He will answer you. Thank you very much."[15]

After the auditorium emptied out, the Family piled into McDonald's and ate everything they had. The invasion comprised well over 200 Family members—singers, dancers, Korean-Family dignitaries, Oakland-Berkeley folks, and one of Father's 70-member "International One World Crusade" teams.

And that night I encountered the warm, fatherly side of the powerful Sun Myung Moon. He sang for us with great smiles and sparkling eyes and even danced a little. Then True Mother sang like an opera star and I realized she was one of the most beautiful Oriental women I had ever seen.

What did *I* think about Sun Myung Moon? I had seen enough. In a letter to my buddy Jim Britt, dated February 3, 1974, I told him—This is the guy I was telling you about, the guy who is supposed to have attained that level of "perfection" and oneness with God. . . . Well I'm going to stick around and see what Reverend Moon has in store for this world.

Chapter Ten

Shipped Out

It was April 23, 1974. The Oakland-Berkeley Family was huddled in the cavernous dining room of our new $250,000 center on Hearst Street, a stately fraternity house bordering the Berkeley campus. After the morning prayer Luke bounced onto his lean, spry legs. "Brothers and Sisters, we have exciting news! Father called Onni last night, and he needs 30 top members for the International One World Crusade (IOWC) teams. *Immediately*. Onni and the staff prayed deeply in deciding who would go on this mission."

Luke began reading off the names of the chosen 30 over the tense, excited jabber. I didn't listen very closely since I was a full-time student in the middle of my third quarter. Suddenly I heard "Steve Kemperman." Luke might as well have hit me in the chest with a concrete block. I thought—*What! How could Onni have the gall to take me out of school?! I'm smack in the middle of my last freshman quarter and she didn't even bother to discuss this with me!* I was going to protest.

When they drafted three more students including Sandra, the Berkeley law student, I knew I was in trouble. Then Daniel took Sandra and me aside and made short work of my protests. He put his hands on our shoulders and said, "I know, I know. I think school is very important too. But Onni prayed about it and I prayed about it and I know this mission is your chance to make a real sacrifice for God and the True Parents. Heavenly Father really needs you and wants you to go."

I felt like a stampeding grizzly bear who'd just been shot and tranquilized into a mound of quivering, helpless flesh. Bludgeoned by guilt and shame. How could I tell the Brothers and

Sisters, "Well, you guys go ahead and work on the IOWC for the Messiah and world restoration, but I have more important things to do here at school."

I withdrew from UC Berkeley that afternoon and spent the next seven days in an intensive training program—full-time fund-raising and witnessing in the Bay area and a smasher workshop at Booneville.

Half the pioneers, including myself, were marked for Dr. Bernhart's IOWC in Boston, the other half for Boulder, Colorado. Christine told us we'd return in four months. But I knew this was just a line to quiet the trembling hearts of the younger members. Once you were shipped out on pioneer mission you never came back.

That week I wallowed in depression. I realized I might never see Berkeley again. As for thoughts of not returning to college, I loved school too much to even allow such considerations. What was happening to my life? I had moved in with the Family as a student who planned to spend four years in Berkeley working for a college degree. Now I was being dispatched to the other side of the continent, to an unknown destiny.

Two days before we left, Christine told me Onni wanted the student members to return to school in the fall and that I should make this clear to my IOWC commander. I sprinted through that day like a jailbird gone free. I was coming back!

But I felt sorry for the others, especially the younger members. In order to keep her longtime members, Onni was sending out three- and five-week members, young people clearly shaken and confused by this business of being shipped off to Timbuktu only weeks after having met the group. I tried to rationalize this ruthless, unfeeling streak in the great Onni, but couldn't.

On Thursday, May 2, 1974 the "Oakland Thirty" piled into a caravan of station wagons and vans and roared out across America towards the rising of the sun and our misty fates.

On May 8, fifteen of us marched up the steps of the Boston Center into a melee of cheering, whistling Unification Church members from the four corners of the earth. Our International One World Crusade commander, Dr. Bernhart, greeted us at the door with tender warmth. What a shiny little character:

diamond-bright eyes, curly brush-wire hair and boyish features. So this was the young medical doctor who'd closed his practice in Colorado and gone traveling to eventually meet the Family in Berkeley?

The IOWC was a recruiting arm of the Unification Church comprising ten 70-member teams working ten five-state regions. Our New England IOWC included members from Japan, America, Scotland, Ireland, Britain, Austria, France and Germany.

Jumping from full-time academia into full-time fund-raising and witnessing was as shocking as leaping into an ice-cold lake. Fund-raising entailed selling candy or flowers for ten hours a day at parking lots and traffic signals. Witnessing entailed approaching young people at public hot-spots like the Boston Commons, the Public Garden or Harvard Square and at college campuses—Tufts, Harvard, Brandeis, Boston College, Northeastern, Boston University. Sometimes we staged rallies—singing, lecturing from charts, and speaking extemporaneously with megaphones.

In Berkeley I'd represented "The New Education Development," I now represented "The International One World Crusade," or sometimes "The Unified Family" (the nomen more commonly used by the European Family). Father was also initiating official recruiting chapters for college and high-school campuses—the Collegiate Association for the Research of Principles (C.A.R.P.) and the Highschool Association for the Research of Principles (H.A.R.P.). We were a movement of many.

On witnessing days I approached young people on park benches, in student lounges and cafeterias, etc. The goal was to bring them back to dinner at the center. Our main recruiting technique consisted of sounding out people's interests and saying, "Wow. That's exactly what *we're* into!" I'd tell liberal long-hairs that I lived in a commune. I'd tell cultural intellectuals about the international aspect of our group and invite them to a free dinner at our "International Night."

Our somewhat deceitful fund-raising and recruiting styles were commonly known in the Unification Church as "heavenly deception." Father once said: "Evil has deceived goodness into evil, but goodness has not been able to deceive evil into goodness. This must be the reason why Christianity couldn't accomplish God's will, until today."[16] So with the appearance of the "New Christianity" (the Family), adept at deceiving evil into goodness, God's will could finally be accomplished.

June, 1974

Today I sold at an intersection in Deadham at an island where two roads crossed. I ran from one red light to another in my flashy purple tie, yellow shirt and vest with my gleaming white new tennis shoes streaking over the ground. . . . Fund-raising is such a growing trial but well worth the suffering and hardship when you look back on it. . . . It was so hard to love people today, so financially I did pretty bad! . . . How can I make that connection with your heart, heavenly Father, so that the good spirit world can work through me?

Often I hear songs on the car radios and they usually bring back memories of nostalgic pastimes. "Has anybody seen my old friend Bob?" So I modified it to, "Has anybody seen my old friend Jim?" because I was thinking of Jim Britt. . . . In a way it made my heart open, which was good, but in a way it was satanic because it made me center on my deviated past.

June, 1974

I sold at the same intersection in Deadham today. . . . I cried once because I was getting so much negativity from people in the cars. Not because it hurt me personally so much, but because I could see their satanic nature exhibiting itself. I stood in the grassy traffic island and looked at a far-off mountain and let the tears roll down my face. . . . Thanks for a growing day, Father.

No, I wasn't too happy with my new life-style of fund-raising or "witnessing" day after endless day. In the first place, there was the constant rejection and fatigue. (My sleep had been cut to four hours a night.) But there was something else. How strange it was to run around representing the Messiah's movement and not be able to freely and honestly tell people what we *really* believed and what our *actual* activities and goals were. Even if heavenly deception was an accepted and common practice in the Family, I still didn't feel good about it. Whether fund-raising or witnessing, I fluctuated constantly between confident exhilaration at giving folks an opportunity to support or even follow the Messiah, and distracting guilt for deceiving people into thinking we were a Christian counseling group, a missionary crusade, or an international community movement.

When the guilt or fatigue began crashing in over the gunwales, I'd stop to pray for inspiration and strength. Sometimes flashes of confusion hit me so hard that for several seconds I didn't know whether I was a member of the Messiah's family or of the ecumenical social movement I was portraying to the public!

Now that I was no longer a freewheeling student but rather an around-the-clock worker in the Unification Church, I began experiencing the full impact of the group's principle of "following center man." The Divine Principle teaches that God works through the "central figure." In practice this means that your immediate superior's actions and words are directly guided by God. The gist of this principle is that if you support your leader, no matter how absurd his actions and words may seem, God can work through him and realize His will. That's why Unification Church leaders are always harping—"Don't *question*. Don't be *arrogant! Follow center man!*" Also, by following center man or "serving the 'Abel Position' " Family members can overcome arrogant satanic nature and grow spiritually. This principle of "heavenly authority" helps create within the Unification Church an incredibly powerful, rigid and effective chain of command which flows from Sun Myung Moon all the way down to the lowliest fund-raiser. The first morning after I was "promoted" to assistant under group leader Don Zapata, Don chewed me out for not serving his breakfast. So I fetched his breakfast. Then when I started into my bowl of Captain Crunch, Don chided me for eating before *he'd* started eating.

"Let's get this straight," he barked. "Center man is the *first* to be served, and center man is the *first* to eat." Some of Zapata's group members took notes on his morning pep talks as if

69367

he were the reincarnation of the prophet Isaiah! (It wasn't long though before I was scribbling along with the rest of them.)

No, I didn't like what had happened to me. When I'd "joined" the movement I never realized I might be sent away to other parts of the Family to spend entire days selling and recruiting. But I accepted my fate because I couldn't turn my back on the truth, on the Messiah. Even my Dutch ancestors were counting on me! No matter how painful all this was, I saw no other recourse but to grit my teeth and follow, and hope the world would hurry up and get restored.

From week number one I was shocked at how different the national Unification Church was from the Oakland-Berkeley group. We California members had always perceived ourselves as a social movement, while the rest of the American Family perceived itself as "The Unification Church"—a church of young missionaries. And perhaps this distinction partially explained why the national Church was lacking in Oakland-Berkeley's high spirit and bold enthusiasm (and why a disproportionately large percentage of Unification Church members join in California).

We were a newly formed and novice IOWC and of course needed time to organize and adjust. But the longer I stayed with IOWC No. 10, the more disillusioned I became with it. Our team's performance was up and down to say the least. One week the group would seem united and effective; but a week later we'd be wallowing in apathy and "spiritual problems"— members constantly falling asleep in fetal prayer positions, or sleeping the day away behind shopping centers or in parks.

And I wasn't the only Oakland-Berkeley member disillusioned with the Unification Church outside California. Our fourth day in Boston, kindhearted Bart Simpson got so fed up with the low energy and the low standard of love and service that he hitchhiked back to the California Family.

In terms of recruitment, we were failing horribly. After an entire month we'd attracted only four new members. The leaders began chastising us, saying we were failing because of our lack of unity and because our hearts weren't right. Then the situation seemed to worsen instead of improve. I worried about the spiritual welfare of members like Francois, the Frenchman, who were so crushed by the IOWC grind that they wandered apathetically through each day like drugged animals.

In June, strange things began happening. Our cook, Rhonda, threw a fit, a spiritual breakdown of sorts. When the police arrived to take her to the hospital she looked so gaunt and spaced they presumed she was on drugs. That same week a brand new female member "freaked out" during the evening program. She tore into the backyard like a terrified, squawking bird and began screaming hideously. We assumed she'd been possessed by an evil spirit and finally had to drag her to a car and drive her home. Whatever caused these bizarre occurrences, it didn't say much for IOWC No. 10.

Then who of all people should visit me that spring but my own mom and dad! As we waited in the vestibule for Dr. Bernhart, Mom kept staring at the Brothers and Sisters milling around in the living room. Suddenly she leaned close to Dad's ear and whispered, "Joop, they all look retarded!"

At first I thought, "Satan! He's invading my mother's thoughts!" Then Francois slouched by with a lifeless stare in his eyes and I winced. Darn! My mother had detected the very spacey quality of our novice IOWC. *O heavenly Father! I'm in God's true Family and I'm ashamed. Why isn't the rest of the Unification Church like Oakland? What's going on?*

After two very awkward days, my parents returned to Rochester, not very impressed with Sun Myung Moon's Unification Church.

None of this made much sense to me. I couldn't understand how the spiritless and zonked-out IOWC No. 10 could even *exist* in the movement of the Lord of the Second Advent! In Berkeley I'd been fairly inspired about bringing guests to our lively evening programs. Now I felt blocked from drawing people into the family of God, almost ashamed to bring young people to the center. And to my own surprise, when someone joined the Family, I felt sorry for the guy. He had no idea what was in store for him. In the end, my three-month IOWC experience confused me terribly, and seriously hampered my faith in the True Parents and the Family for years to come.

Chapter Eleven

Politics, Politics, Politics

*" 'Tis time to fear when
tyrants seem to kiss,"*
William Shakespeare, Pericles

Father had always made it clear that Jesus failed His mission because He never gained the support of the Jewish leaders. To win over the majority, the masses, you have to first win over the leadership. Father also said, "Let's say there are 500 sons and daughters like you in each state. Then we could control the government. You could determine who became senators and who the congressmen would be."[17]

During my first eight months in the Family I participated in two of Sun Myung Moon's campaigns organized to woo the support and endorsement of national leaders. In June, 1974 IOWC No. 10 enthusiastically and very visibly supported the campaign to elect Congressman Louis Wyman of New Hampshire as U.S. senator. We pasted bumper stickers on pro-Wyman cars, hoping he would be elected and remember that we had put him in office. Then during our trek to Boston in May the Oakland Thirty and Mr. Weinar's IOWC rallied in support of President Richard Nixon when he spoke in Phoenix. Nixon was flailing in tempestuous political seas whipped up by the Watergate scandal. We wanted and needed his support, and believed we could get it by helping to save his presidency. It seemed Sun Myung Moon was determined not to make the same mistake Jesus had made.

Along with our political activities came the constant barrage of bold political themes which streaked the fiber of the Divine Principle and Sun Myung Moon's speeches. All this seemed to add up to one thing—comprising the very core of

Unification Church ideology and practice was not simply the pursuit of the "spiritual life," but also politics, politics and more politics.

In November, 1973 Sun Myung Moon launched an open, all-out campaign to keep President Richard M. Nixon in the White House. On November 30, Father issued a statement entitled "Forgive, Love, Unite" to 21 major newspapers across the nation. In it Father said that the solution to the Watergate crisis, which was rocking America with bitterness, hatred and the beginnings of destruction, was to forgive, love and unite around our President. On December 11, 1973 Richard Nixon sent Sun Myung Moon a statement of appreciation for our support.

Father immediately ordered centers around the country to send members to Washington, D.C. to rally in front of the White House. Two-and-a-half days later Fred Seymour, Jacob and other Oaklanders screeched off the turnpike into the capital city. Hundreds of Family members were jostling in the park across from the White House—chanting pep slogans, singing "God Bless America," and brandishing picket signs reading "God Loves Nixon!"; "Support the President"; and "Forgive, Love, Unite!"

That morning Tricia Nixon Cox and her husband slipped out of the White House and mingled with the Family. At 11:00 P.M. Family members were still rallying and singing and jumping around to stay warm when a brother started yelling "The President! . . . It's the President!"

Richard Nixon crossed the street with two secret service men and was swallowed up in a sea of ecstatic Unification Church members. Nixon chatted for 15 minutes before he returned to the White House. Afterwards, Mr. Salonen mentioned that he saw tears in Nixon's eyes. Two days later Sun Myung Moon was granted an audience with the President. Our leader embraced him, urged him to remain strong and in office, and prayed fervently in Korean as Nixon listened in silence.

That year the Family staged rally after rally in support of President Nixon, not only in the States but overseas as well. Everywhere Nixon went the Family was sure to go. Whenever he spoke in public, Family members bounced in the bleachers and on the sidewalks, waving banners proclaiming "Support the President!" and cheering, "God loves Nixon! . . . God loves Nixon!" We were working hard for his support of the Unification Church.

On August 8, 1974 Richard Nixon resigned as President of the United States. It was a terrible tragedy for the providence of God in America. At first I saw Nixon as a complete fool and felt bitter towards him for having given up the fight. But two days after his resignation Father explained, "I am sure there is a communist power working behind the scenes. They came to threaten to kill him if he did not resign, and that's what compelled him to do so."[18] Yet the most tragic aspect of this failure was not that America had lost a president, but that the Lord of the Second Advent had lost the most important and powerful potential ally he had ever had.

The Family's loathing for communism was nothing less than blood-red serious. In June of 1975 Sun Myung Moon staged a pro-government rally in South Korea and pledged to more than one million people that in the event of an invasion from North Korea, Unification Church members would come from the four corners of the earth to fight the communist power.

According to the *Divine Principle*, the seeds of communism and democracy were planted with the birth of Cain and Abel. Here, two lines of philosophy formed. The lineage of Cain, who was the fruit of Eve's love relationship with Satan,* culminated in communism. The lineage of Abel, who was the fruit of Eve's love relationship with Adam, culminated in democracy. So communism is the expression of Satan, and democracy is the expression of God. Satan strives for world dominion through the communist nations, and God works to realize *His* kingdom through the democratic nations.

In this struggle between God and Satan, Korea stands as the chosen nation of God—the birthplace of the Messiah, the Holy Land of the worldwide Family, the first nation which will

---

* Genesis 4:1 flatly states that Cain was the result of intercourse between Adam and Eve, not Lucifer and Eve.

see perfection. The thirty-eighth parallel separating North and South Korea is literally the front line between God and Satan. South Korea must be protected at all costs from a communist takeover. If the communists overrun it, the hope of human salvation will be annihilated. In the course of restoration, communism *must* be destroyed, either on the ideological level or in a third world war.

However, the base of world restoration is not Korea, but rather America. Being the leading democratic nation and founded on Christian principles, God has chosen America as the nation around which all others will unite.

The American arm of Father's battle against communism is the Freedom Leadership Foundation (FLF). It is based in Washington, D.C., and among other activities publishes the Family's anti-communist newspaper, *The Rising Tide*. In Japan, the Family's "International Federation of Victory over Communism" (IFVC) is actively supported and financially backed by prominent political figures and wealthy Japanese industrialists. Kishi Nobusake, prime minister of Japan from 1957 to 1961, presently heads the organization.

Sun Myung Moon and church leaders often used the "threat of communism" theme to inspire us to action. As I grew older in the Family my political views changed drastically and a determination to annihilate the forces of satanic communism became a great source of inspiration for my work.

I'll never forget Aaron O'Brian's mesmerizing/terror-filled speech on the imminent communist threat. The Irishman performed at a microphone before 2,000 Family members crammed into the main ballroom of the New Yorker Hotel, the worldwide headquarters of the Unification Church. At one point he flung his arms downward and yelled, "The complete and total defeat of communism is *essential* for world restoration! America is God's *hope*, the only nation in the world capable of standing up against the communist powers. If America falls to the communists, the world is *doomed!* . . . Doomed to a living hell of communist rule for centuries to come!"

O'Brian then described a Family member's dream about how the communist armies swept into New York City after the U.S. was defeated in World War III. Buildings burned, crowds stampeded, firing squads first executed Family members then ordinary citizens. We envisioned the scenario with wild, gaping eyes.

Towards the close of the speech O'Brian began rallying us to "Victory over Communism!" "Victory over Satan!" At that point they could have put guns in our hands and marched us off to war! We wouldn't have thought twice about killing a red.

Then we scrambled to our feet and the Irishman cranked a fist back and bellowed, "We pledge *VICTORY* for our True Parents and heavenly Father! . . . Abojeeeeeee [father]!"

Then 2,000 pairs of fists shot into the air with one voice of thunder, "Manseeeeeeeeei!" Then again, "Abojeeeee! Manseeeeeeei! Abojeeeeee! Manseeeeeeeei!"

The endorsements of prominent politicians were invaluable since they boosted the public image of the Unification Church. Basically, we had three methods by which we compiled our list of "supporters." One method consisted of having mayors and governors sign proclamations to honor Sun Myung Moon's Day of Hope Tour. Our big catches here were Governor Jimmy Carter and Governor George Wallace. A second method was using, in our PR material, the names of prominent figures who attended Father's Day of Hope Banquets. And the third method—over the years our leader managed to get himself photographed shaking hands with such well-known figures as former President Eisenhower and Senators Hubert Humphrey, James L. Buckley, Strom Thurmond and Edward Kennedy. Of course most of this name-gathering occurred before anyone had heard much about Sun Myung Moon and the Unification Church.

Another ambitious program was Father's lobbying effort on Capitol Hill. At a directors' conference in 1973, Sun Myung Moon informed the leadership that "Master [Father] needs many good-looking girls. We will assign three girls to one senator—that means three hundred. Let them have a good relationship with them. One is for the election, one is to be the diplomat, and one is for the party. If our girls are superior to the senators in many ways, then the senators will be taken in by our members."[19] Since 1973 PR Sisters and Brothers have worked hard at lobbying for such issues as continued military aid to South Korea and at promoting a positive image of the

Unification Church among our nation's legislators.

There was certainly no question as to whether or not Sun Myung Moon supported President Park Chung Hee and the South Korean government. The Unification Church responded to criticism about its support of the Park government with the argument that, though Park operated a dictatorial regime, he maintained a strong and united front against a possible invasion from the north. Democracy was a luxury South Korea could not afford.

Sun Myung Moon's campaign against communism had helped him gain the favor and support of the South Korean government. Father had established the International Federation for Victory over Communism in Korea as well as a school outside Seoul which offered training in the techniques of anti-communism. Each year the government sent thousands of civilian officials and military personnel to participate in the school's program.

In the mid 1970s the Unification Church became entangled in a scandal with the Korean Central Intelligence Agency (KCIA). The KCIA's harassment of Korean Americans reached such serious proportions in 1973 that the State Department ordered an FBI investigation of KCIA activities in the United States. Later Colonel Bo Hi Pak was implicated in the scandal. He had been assistant military attaché for the South Korean Embassy in Washington, D.C. when he was pioneer-evangelizing for the Family in 1961. Colonel Pak had also helped escort KCIA director Kim Jong Pil on his 1962 tour of the U.S. intelligence community.

So now Korean émigrés and others were asserting that Colonel Pak maintained close ties with the KCIA. Allegations spread that the KCIA was using Sun Myung Moon's movement to further the ends of the Park regime.

For awhile I considered allegations of KCIA-Unification Church collaboration absurd. Yet, after the controversy had been raging for almost a year, I began harboring doubts. So many affairs occurring at the top levels of the Family were steeped in secrecy. Usually not until a controversial aspect of our church appeared in the newspapers would leaders bother explaining things to the rank-and-file membership. This held true for the allegations of communal sex and secret sexual rites of the early days as well as for the evidence that the Korean Family's "Tong-il Industries" was a major producer of military weapons (among them the M-16 rifle and the M-79 grenade launcher).[20]

I was present at the New Yorker Hotel when Father admitted that we did have contracts with the South Korean government to manufacture defense weaponry, but only because South Korean law required it. Then I began realizing that allegations of KCIA involvement might hold more truth than I dared imagine.

Father was always clear about God's ultimate goal of restoration—that one day all nations of the world would follow him and realize a one-world family under God—global theocracy guided by heaven through God's perfect son, Sun Myung Moon.

Our leader proclaimed in 1974 that, "The time will come, without my seeking it, when my words will almost serve as law. If I ask a certain thing to be done, it will be done. If I don't want something, it will not be done."[21]

I often dreamed of going to Africa or South America to help in the restoration of a country. It was an incredible source of hope that one day all peoples would believe in Sun Myung Moon and work together to build a perfect world. Father seemed to be a man quite capable of winning the nations over to his side. Already he had numerous economic and political connections which extended from South Korea to Japan to the United States.

Chapter Twelve

Flowers, Candles, Candy

*"Just as war is waged with the
blood of others, fortunes are
made with other people's money,"*
André Suarès.

One July night, after three months on the IOWC, Dr. Bernhart took me out on the porch and broke the news—I had been chosen for a "six-month mission" on the national Mobile Fundraising Teams (MFT).

"But what about school? Onni said I was going back to Berkeley in the fall."

The IOWC commander then described the fantastic spiritual training the fighting MFT offered, and added, "School can wait; it's only a six-month mission. You can return to school afterwards." By this time I was so used to being shuffled around like a piece on a Monopoly board that I just gave in and assumed it was all God's will!

At the break of dawn they chauffeured me to the airport. I waved good-bye to my sleeping Brothers and Sisters and to my sweet "spiritual mother" Arlane who stood crying on the sidewalk. From Boston I flew to Youngstown, Ohio to rendezvous with my team captain, Duane Jimson. Duane's seven-man team was gypsying around eastern and central Ohio in a travel trailer which they parked in private campgrounds.

The MFT was Sun Myung Moon's network of crack, financial green berets. "The backbone of the Unification Church," Father often said. The dozens of teams which worked every state in the nation raised millions each year to finance Father's personal estate and his countless campaigns and projects, real estate purchases being a major beneficiary. Local state centers also trundled in millions annually through fund-raising, selling ginseng tea, and operating small businesses. At this time the East Coast fishing business was just getting started.

At first I was terrified. I'd heard chilling stories about the boot-camp regimen of the MFT. Well, our team *did* operate like a front-lines commando squad. But the teams' positive, fighting, gung-ho spirit was a welcome change from the frustrating and grotesque spaciness of the IOWC. And Duane was a good, tough, but warmhearted leader—a former college student from Des Moines with stabbing dark brown eyes and a bulldog nose above the scar of a cleft palate.

At 5:30 A.M. of my first day on the MFT, after four hours sleep, Duane began stalking through the dark trailer. (The Sisters slept in the van.) "Wake up time!" he growled. Brothers were sardined in bunks, on the floor and under the table. Groan. I dragged my body out of the sleeping bag and began squirming through the crowded stuffy trailer.

After washing-up and morning chores the team trooped into the Dodge van and roared off to Youngstown. As the summer corn and pasture flitted by outside the windows, the Sisters served a turkey-vegetable casserole and orange juice. Soon the Youngstown steel mills and factories loomed in the distance like H.G. Wells's Martian monsters. I began loathing the idea of jumping out to face the public all day, and wished the van would keep rolling down the highway and never stop!

Our captain pulled into a K-Mart parking lot along a road studded with car dealerships, gas stations and McDonald's and Arby's-type food stands. After Duane's fiery pep talk we bowed our heads and prayed that God would bless the area and the people, and mobilize the spirit world to inspire people to buy. We closed this benediction with the cries and moans of unison prayer.

"This is your area, Steve," said Duane. My stomach turned upside down. But I managed to crawl out through my terror onto the asphalt parking lot. Jumping into this shop-to-shop area armed with a box of scented candles felt like parachuting into cannibal-infested jungles with a cub scout knife. (Even after months of fund-raising this first step usually brought on hopeless nausea.) As Duane zoomed away, my teammates shrieked a supportive cheer, "Manseeeeeeeeeei Steeeve! Cruuuuuuuuuushshsh Satan!"

In the morning and afternoon I galloped along suburban highways from appliance store to donut shop to gas station. Then Duane picked me up and after a quick dinner of macaroni and cheese he dropped me in a mall parking lot where I chased exiting shoppers all evening. At ten o'clock I was picked up for "the blitz." Blitzing was hit-and-run fund-raising. Without asking permission, we'd stroll into bars and other nightspots and sell as many flowers or candles as possible before the manager discovered the penetration and booted us out.

Duane gathered up the team around 1:30 A.M. as the bars started closing. What a relief! The day was finally over. As the van bowled along "home" we counted our thick wads of bills and handfuls of coin, joked, sang and shared the day's crazy experiences. A few of the sellers had broken the $300 and $400 mark; I had made a satisfying $183. Back at the campground we huddled near the barbed-wire fence of a farmer's cornfield and bawled a unison prayer into the starry night, thus ending a 20-hour day.

There were few deviations from this basic fund-raising schedule. On weeknights we only worked till midnight and on Sundays we went door-to-door till 9:00 P.M. On the whole, my first day on the MFT involved a routine which became for me a life structure, a pattern as absolute and predictable as the rising of the sun and the changing of the season. Day after day, week after week, month after month—always the same.

After a few weeks in eastern Ohio we hitched up the trailer and moved into the hilly Pennsylvania towns around Pittsburgh. By this time I'd gained enough confidence and selling expertise so that fund-raising was more than just gruelling. It was also pockmarked with adventure.

I enjoyed meeting the American people in their own habitats—the 16-year-old in his jacked-up Chevy roadster, the lawyer in his office, the working woman grinding her factory machine. I usually met them with a sincere heart and a sunny grin—the Messiah's missionary coming not to sell but to give people an opportunity to realize their own salvation. Many reacted with cold disinterest, but others with smiles, laughter and generosity, saying, "Hey, kid, you make it hard to say no!"

But late-night blitzing was better than anything else. Sometimes I'd joke an entire row of bar-stooled patrons into buying $20 worth of flowers or candles.

> August, 1974
>
> At night I did the steep hillside of an intersection (Rte. 8) after nine warnings by McAndless police. . . . It was a lot of fun, people whipping out dollar bills because I was really directing my spirit and love to them.
>
> I did Murphy's and a bar-restaurant in the mall and sold out (except for a couple raunchy flowers which I sold to a lady for fifty cents). Then my bucket got stolen. It was such an exciting night. And it was so great getting so many funny responses from people. . . . One guy bought a white carnation and ate it.
>
> I needed $18 to reach my goal of $200 at 10:50 P.M. Bar by bar, Arby's by Lum's, Ponderosa Steak House by Burger King, flower by flower, I finally sold enough to reach my goal.
>
> After preparing the trailer for our next move, . . . we went to bed at 5:35 A.M. Now we're off to new adventures of the heart!

Of course people rarely knew they were contributing to the Unification Church. They thought they were giving to "Christian counseling centers" or "drug centers." We reasoned that by recruiting people onto the path to perfection we really *were* giving them Christian counseling and "solving their emotional and drug problems."

And I'd gradually lost all my qualms about the role of heavenly deception in the Unification Church. Fund-raising deception is especially justifiable because the donor grows spiritually and also sets a good condition which enables the good spirit world to lead him and his entire lineage to God's Family.

Ever since Theresa and Ollie (two high-selling Sisters) had taught me the art of sneaking into factories and office complexes, I vowed to become a master undercover fund-raiser. In the Pittsburgh steel mills I slipped in back doors, my candy box covered with a sweater. I usually tried to snatch a hard hat, more as a disguise than as protection against the spewing metal and hot ash. The working men couldn't have cared if I was an industrial spy as long as I had peanut brittle or "Turtles." But whenever a white-collared foreman or executive came in sight I casually strode on in my shirt and tie like an office clerk toting supplies.

In high-security office buildings I pretended I was James Bond infiltrating communist headquarters. One flower-selling day I was trying to crack the Pennsylvania Power Company headquarters. Security guards at every door. So I began chatting with a woman executive out front on the sidewalk. She thought I was an employee and together we gabbed right past the security guard into the elevator. Fifteen minutes later a female voice crackled over the PA system: "Will the young man selling flowers please leave the premises." The carnations were selling well so I started skipping floors to confuse my trail. Forty minutes and $35 later a sweating, wheezing, uniformed gorilla cornered me in a Xerox copy room. They decided not to press charges. But once in a while sneaking Brothers and Sisters were arrested, especially when they were slinking around towns which had refused us fund-raising permission.

Successful fund-raising and this brazen disregard for "worldly laws" required a certain mentality or state of mind—complete and absolute conviction that we were the only ones doing God's will on the earth, and the world's *only* hope. This conviction was also tinged with some contempt for Satan's world and its people. No matter what tactics we used we were simply taking money from Satan and giving it back to God. In other words, we believed we were above the laws of men.

In September we rolled into lovely West Virginia—enchanting land of deep "hollers" (valleys), coal miners and mountain men. By this time I would let nothing, absolutely nothing, stop me from reaching my daily financial goal ($200-$300). Nothing phased me. Not kick-outs by shopping center managers or factory foremen, nor the first warnings of local police. If a company's first warning was mild I'd sneak right back into the complex. If the company official bellowed and shivered with rage and threatened to press charges if he caught me again, I'd move on unphased, sometimes even chuckling.

Maintaining this frame of mind, this awareness that I was working for the last Messiah, was difficult and required certain "psyche-up techniques." Occasionally, I'd visualize Sun Myung Moon selling alongside me. Knowing how Father would smile and love the people and tear around the place gave me strength and inspiration. The most effective technique however was chanting. As I sprinted over parking lots or as I crept through noisy factories I chanted: "Two-hundred-and-fifty dollars for Father now! $250 for Father now!" Or, "I will die for God, I will die for the True Parents. I will give my life to reach the goal."

My fund-raising experiences penetrated 14 states and every kind of "area" imaginable. No stronghold was immune to the sales pitch of this Unification Church fund-raising desperado; not the gambling back room of West Virginia bars nor the x-rated back seats of Ohio drive-in theaters. I sold my wares in morgues, health spas, circuses, hospitals, textile factories, U.S. naval bases, football and baseball games, roughhouse and gay bars, racetracks, funeral homes, massage parlors and brothels. You name it, I was there coaxing handouts for the New Messiah.

> November 26, 1974
> A time of struggle has come. Financially I'm doing
> O.K., spiritually I'm not. I have in me a deep desire to
> go back to Oakland. . . . Is it selfish? Perhaps even
> Satan inspired? I just don't know.

When Father spoke at Madison Square Garden in New York, September, 1974 I tracked down Christine and asked her to ask Onni if she could have me sent back to Berkeley in January, in time for UC Berkeley's winter term. She said she would. In November I heard that I was readmitted to Berkeley, but still no word from Christine.

By late November I was worn out and fed up with the mindless fund-raising grind. Finally, one night in early December I plodded in off the freezing parking lot and called California from a Burger King.

"Christine? Did you ask Onni yet?"

"Yes, Stevie. She says you can come back to Oakland if you really want to and if it's OK with your MFT leaders."

After holstering the phone receiver I groaned. Then I shuffled out the door into the biting wind, and into the woods. There, I agonized and prayed into the bleak night.

Onni and her right-hand person had duped me with the same line about returning to California following a "temporary mission." (Dr. Bernhart's "six-month" mission also turned out to be somewhat fictitious.) All along I'd been led to believe that Onni would issue the order to have me return to Berkeley. That none of the student members had returned to school so far only intensified the helpless feeling.

There was no way in Hades that my iron-minded gung-ho regional commander Keith Karl or President Salonen (Keith's superior) would allow me to revert to college/center life. It was out of the question! As far as I knew, outside Oakland no full-fledged member attended college. And *demanding* my transfer was impossible. A mountain of guilt blocked the way back to the land of sunshine. Leaving the respected MFT against the will of my central figure would be outright desertion, abandoning the front line mission during time of war.

I stood in the dark, snowy woods with the clenching wind and the moaning trees and cried—my great hope of returning to the life of learning I loved so much was finally smothered forever. And like flashes of soundless summer lightning, the realization penetrated that I'd been *deceived* in Oakland. They never told me that I might be sent out to fund-raise day after windswept day in snow-clogged parking lots, trudging, shivering, pushing on. My close-knit community of warmhearted idealists had mutated into a harsh, militaristic political/religious movement. I had been "heavenly deceived" into following the thorny and tearstained path of the Messiah.

The privilege of being able to pioneer-follow the second Christ seemed minor and insignificant compared to the aching sadness and dread which filled my soul. Finally, I realized that if I had known that life in the Family would come to this, would often drag into something akin to the hopeless, futureless and tearfilled life of a slave—I would never have become part of Sun Myung Moon's Unification Church. I realized all this, felt fully helpless, and wept.

Chapter Thirteen

Doubts

"Let the brothers ever avoid appearing gloomy, sad, and clouded, like the hypocrites; but let one ever be found joyous in the Lord, gay, amiable, gracious, as is meet,"
Saint Francis of Assisi.

I stood on the wintry mountainside and watched the black clouds sweep eastward. That night North Carolina seemed as cold as upstate New York. As my hands clutched a photograph of Sun Myung Moon and Hak Ja Han, I started praying and trying to visualize the True Parents standing next to me. So began a new battle for my spiritual well-being.

The last MFT reshuffling in January, 1975 had landed me on Peter Sasano's team in western North Carolina. During my first months on the MFT the incredible variety of scenarios and people had filled each day with surprise, novelty and adventure. But by now I'd worked almost every kind of area so many times that the novelty and excitement had worn off. Fund-raising had become a gruelling and mindless dawn-to-midnight grind. And to muster the strength and inspiration I needed to keep going, I had thrown myself into developing a spiritual relationship with the True Parents.

The Parents (especially Father) had completely replaced Jesus as the sole mediator between God and man. Learning to love Sun Myung Moon and Hak Ja Han would establish an incredibly powerful relationship with God. In fact, Father said that we should have many dreams about the True Parents and experience a deep spiritual life with them. The spirit of the True Parents is everywhere. Therefore if we love the Parents so much that we miss them and want to be with them, they will come to us in our thoughts, in visions and in dreams.

Yet, though I was pouring my energies into developing this relationship with the holy couple, almost every time I tried to visualize the True Parents the sunny faces of Mom and Dad would tune in. I began feeling guilty and disturbed that I loved my physical mother and father more than the true Lord and His bride. I feared that this earthly love was seriously blocking my spiritual growth. A Unification Church member is supposed to love the True Parents more than anyone in the world, even more than his natural parents. So that night I vowed to myself and the chill, lonely mountain that I would learn to love True Mother and Father more than my own Mom and Dad.

In May, 1975 I decided it was high time to visit my physical family, though I had mixed feelings about such a visit. On the one hand, I didn't look forward to putting up with their negative attitude towards the Church. On the other hand Mom and Dad treated me with a great deal of kindness in spite of their views. And most importantly, I relished the three- or four-day break from fund-raising as a desert trekker relishes a cool glass of water.

The past months had been particularly unpleasant. Half the team constantly struggled with spiritual problems, and that winter Peter had enforced a four-minute cold shower indemnity condition in the unheated campground bathrooms.

By this time my connection with the True Parents had greatly improved. The thoughts and feelings of love for Mom and Dad which used to compete with my love for Mother and Father recurred less and less frequently. So when I boarded the plane in Greenville, South Carolina I felt confident that I could admirably represent the True Parents and effectively withstand and counter my physical family's negativity towards the Unification Church.

My first day home Hubert took me to the Sunday service at his church. To my surprise I found an enthusiasm and a strong inspiring spirit I didn't know existed in the Christian churches. The following night Hubert, Mom and I attended an introductory prayer meeting sponsored by a small group of charismatic Catholics. Bob and Judith, a husband and wife team, moderated, with Judith doing most of the talking.

What an incredible life-power this woman radiated! As she spoke of her faith and experiences with God and Jesus I saw a pure love and a quiet, confident strength I hadn't seen anywhere in a long time. When she talked about her Jesus she seemed to be talking about a real person she had met and come to know. And it was clear that she loved her Jesus more than I loved *my* Lord.

To top it off, every few minutes my head slumped onto my chest, overcome by fatigue and sleep. After the meeting I felt crushed with shame. Here I was—the follower of the Christ returned—and not only was I falling asleep but I couldn't even come close to matching this woman's pure faith and shining love.

Though my family had come to strongly disapprove of the Unification Church, no real confrontations materialized during the first few days. Then on the evening of the third day, after dinner, all seven of us sat down in the living room for cake and coffee.

Suddenly Hubert started prying into our teachings on the mission of Jesus. Within minutes Mom, Dad, Hubert and Bruce were all taking turns attacking the Family's beliefs and practices. Had Jesus achieved full salvation through His death on the cross? When I argued that Jesus had not fully completed His mission and mentioned the failure of John the Baptist, the fire went out of control. Hubert jumped for the Bible and I ran upstairs for my *Divine Principle* book.

We debated for three hours, developed breaking-point nerves and achieved absolutely nothing. About the only thing I learned was that my folks believed I was a victim of mind control.

Then Mom brandished a Family publication she had found in my room. "Look at these pictures! How can you believe in these people?" She waved the book in my face and pointed to a picture of the True Father and Mother appearing in public. Mother wore an expensive fur coat, Father looked rather mafioso in his sunglasses, with his hands stuffed in the pockets of a sleek, black coat. "What phonies! All dressed up like movie stars while you kids are running around on the streets in absolute poverty. My God it makes me sick!"

At 3:30 A.M. I stood up, said that I'd had enough and we all stalked off to bed.

Finally, the time came to return to my mission on the MFT. All along Mom and Dad had been trying to keep me from going back to the Unification Church. When I kissed them good-bye and walked onto the runway they looked disappointed and deeply hurt.

I felt I'd admirably defended my commitment to the Unification Church and escaped unscathed. But as the DC-10 sped back to Greenville, a peculiar anxiety and turmoil seeped in and paralyzed me. The anxiety wasn't anything intellectual, just a sickening gut feeling about Sun Myung Moon.

When I stared at the pictures of our leader in a Family paperback called *Christianity in Crisis* I felt nothing for him, absolutely nothing. Many times I had felt a definite warmth or at least a huge admiration for his powerful personality. He was the Messiah, my true spiritual Father who had suffered a thousand times more than Jesus! Now I felt not a trace of love for this man.

My stay in Rochester had shaken my faith so deeply that for three days I actually doubted that Sun Myung Moon was the Messiah. Motivation ebbed and I fought to keep selling, stopping every half hour to pray over my photo of True Father and Mother at Belvedere. I *had* to believe Father was the Messiah. If I didn't I might end up leaving the Family, which was synonymous with spiritual death. And even if I could force myself to stay I would go insane if I didn't believe this most central teaching. Finally after an eternal week of chanting, praying and fending off doubts I regained my faith in the True Father.

After this visit home other doubts about the Unification Church began springing up regularly. Ironically, the most traumatic doubts arose when I started comparing the Unification Church with the Christian faith. Somehow the exposure to the Christian groups in Rochester had sowed a seed of respect and admiration for these ardent followers of the first Son of God.

One of my doubts concerned the born-again Christian movement. Why was it booming, bringing so many people to God when the followers of the True Son of God, Sun Myung

Moon, could barely keep the ranks filled? Considering the millions of dollars and countless man-hours we poured into the American restoration, our growth rate was very poor.

Then new doubts arose after the director of the Barrytown missionary training program, Mr. Ken Sudo, predicted that around the time of Yankee Stadium campaign a great Pentecost would sweep America and that hundreds and thousands would flock to and join the Unification Church. Well, Sudo's Pentecost never materialized.

Though my knowledge of the New Testament was quite minimal, I did know that the first Pentecost represented the visitation of the Holy Spirit to the apostles and that it had been a dramatic and wonderful occasion; and knowing this made the failure of Mr. Sudo's prediction appear even more ludicrous. The book of Acts relates how Peter was filled with the power of the Holy Spirit and spoke to the crowds in Jerusalem. That same day 3,000 people joined the apostles in following the Christ. Three thousand people in one day! The Unification Church had been struggling in the United States since the early sixties and by 1975 had barely mustered 4,000 core members. Because these doubts caused incredible havoc and dissonance in my selling life, I tried desperately to suppress them.

In September, 1975 Peter Sasano's team set up camp in northeastern Tennessee around Bristol and Johnson City. The team's morale ebbed to a depressing low. Some members were spacing out and sleeping through whole selling periods. My heavenly mission and life in general had lost their meaning and I struggled each day just to keep going. Some mornings I woke up in the darkness of that dingy trailer and wished I were dead.

During my first week in Tennessee I discovered a wonderful little Christian book in the trailer called *Prison to Praise,* by Merlin R. Carothers. (Maybe one of the sellers had received it from a church-going shopper or store owner.) Without the inspirational message of this book I would have plunged into severe depression and spaced out like other members.

At night I read the paperback in my bunk, by day I stuffed it in my candy box. *Prison to Praise* presented a theme which gave a purpose and a meaning to that difficult period in my life. It was based on a verse from Romans: "In everything God works for good with those who love him" (8:28). The idea was that if we praise, thank and love God in all our life situations, no matter how trying they may be, God can use those situations to our spiritual benefit.

So I spent my days thanking and praising God for everything I had—my life, my health, the great green Tennessee mountains, the sunny, dewy fields. Because of this great Christian inspiration I was able to go beyond my suffering and love God, and in this way receive His love in return.

There'd been times when I turned only to the literature of the Unification Church to find inspiration. But after a year and a half in the Family both the *Divine Principle* and "Master Speaks" had lost some of their zing. They just didn't give me the same sense of excitement and life as did books by Christians who spoke of how God was working in their lives. Somehow the *Divine Principle* seemed more like a system of formulas. I *did* believe that the D.P. and Father's words represented God's highest truth. But they simply lacked the thrilling hope and joy of the Christian faith.

During one fight-it-out week in South Carolina that August I gave up in despair and spent an entire day in a Methodist church bathroom reading the Gospels. Other times I read books by Corrie Ten Boom: *The Hiding Place* and *Tramp for the Lord.* Sporadically, over the months and years, Christian literature continued to give my life booster shots of meaning and inspiration when everything else failed.

In October 1975 our MFT region gathered for a training session in Kings Mountain, North Carolina. After the workshop we raced off to Washington, D.C. where Father spoke to us on two consecutive days. At the close of this rare five-day vacation, President Salonen reorganized the teams and assigned me to a team bound for Cleveland and headed by Justin Kleinman.

Thick-skinned, industrial Cleveland was a tough fundraising area, but I worked hard and did well. In November Keith Karl transferred our team to Richmond, Virginia. There my troubles began.

December, 1975
Another bummer day. This whole month has been

a seller's nightmare. Not due to any external conditions, mind you, but just a personal lack of motivation and commitment to selling. I've spaced out, fallen
asleep in bathrooms, taken to frequent breaks and
not sold with all my heart and effort for several weeks
now. . . . I've come up with all kinds of different
answers to my problem, mostly a lot of different ways
to inspire myself to sell. All I know is that I have to stop
this pattern of not giving myself completely in my
work.

My bag of psyche-up tricks had run dry. And my sleep-
starved body couldn't propel itself on sheer determination. My
mission, the mission of the Unification Church, seemed like a
paper myth. After two years in the Family I was still running
around selling stuff—bored, empty, and filled with despair.
Every morning when I stepped out of the van, a thousand
atmospheres of hopelessness, fear and wretched sloth came
crashing down on my spirit. And in that state I simply could
not bring myself to fund-raise.

So I'd take cover in a public bathroom, sit down on the pot
and try to pray the monster away. But I always fell asleep. When
I woke it was not to a world of light and sound, but to a dim,
groggy, sickening stupor. And my brain would ring with the
curses and howls of accusing evil spirits. (They would accuse
us in order to drag us into paralyzing guilt and depression.)

"You! You're failing your responsibility! Failing the Messiah. Failing God! Damn you! Damn you!" Terrifying guilt. And
it never let up. These space-outs were more awful than anything I'd ever endured. It would have been less agonizing if I'd
gone stomping on down the road, simply forcing myself to sell.
But I just couldn't go on. I just couldn't.

Such a space-out episode usually lasted an entire four-hour
selling period. Then I'd summon the last shreds of my courage
and determination and push on. Only one thing prevented me
from throwing in the towel—FEAR. I could never forget what
had happened to an all-star fund-raiser named Jim Mathis.
During our Cleveland mission in October, Jim had failed his
mission and been taken off the MFT. He'd burned out.

"Burning out" was a term we used to describe the crushed,

defeated state some members slipped into after years in the Family, especially after several years on the MFT. A burned-out member has virtually no will left, almost as if he doesn't care whether he lives or dies.

The great super-salesman Jim Mathis finally burned out and stopped selling altogether. Within a week Keith Karl transferred him to some obscure mission in New York. When we drove him to the airport he sat slumped in the back seat, his head drooping, dark fleshy rings bulging under the eyes, his once rocky jaw sagging listlessly. What shocked me most was the glazed look in his eyes, as if something within him had died.

After three weeks I finally decided I couldn't endure another day of that harrowing drudgery. One December morning as my team captain crawled out of his sleeping bag I told him I was very sick and needed rest. Justin studied my face for a few seconds. Crippling despair had worked like a disease. I looked emaciated and gaunt—bloodless cheeks and lips, puffy eye-sacks. Without a question or a comment Justin *ordered* me to rest up that day. I breathed sweet relief because most leaders would have pegged my symptoms as the effects of an evil spiritual invasion and told me to get up and "fight it out."

I hadn't faked physical illness just to spare myself the agony of another fund-raising day. Somehow I had to beat this lack of motivation. My strategy—a full day of inspirational reading. We were staying at the Richmond Center and the bookshelves carried a number of books of inspirational value.

After a couple of hours' sleep I spent over ten hours reading several books on the life of Saint Francis of Assisi. That day "God's happy little man" became for me the greatest saint who ever lived. Before this time I'd viewed Christian saints as clay statues with names in religious history books. But the accounts of Francis's life are detailed and vivid. And reading about his youth, aspirations, travels, conversations with God and about Francis's personal wisdom showed me that here was a man who had lived life to its fullest, lived in God, and most of all, a man who had truly loved.

Francis lived within a great circle of love which began with his God, encompassed man and the natural world and ultimately returned to his relationship with the heavenly Father.

He often sought his Lord in the woodlands and flowered fields of his native Italy and the things of God's creation were his own loved ones—"Brother Sun," "Sister Moon," even "Friar Wolf."

He was also a tremendous practical joker and loved to work his gags on the brothers in his following; he disliked the grave, overly solemn piousness many of the religious settled into. He believed in serving God joyfully. This is how he earned the name "God's happy little man." And ultimately Saint Francis loved so much that he revolutionized the lifeless and corrupt church of his day and brought thousands to a new life in the spirit of God's love.

My day of inspirational reading was my salvation. The story of Saint Francis, his example of love for God and men, his incredible faith, and his mirthy joy gave me the hope and strength I needed. In fact, this spiritual booster kept me chugging for a long time.

Yet, strangely I almost envied Saint Francis more than I admired him. I couldn't help notice that our own 24-hour service to God and our incredible sacrifices did not simply flow out of our love for the heavenly Father, out of a great joy of living for Him. To such a large degree our sacrifices were not offered freely but *exacted* of us, driven, squeezed and wrung out of us. And this took all the fun out of living for God.

That night I dreamed for the first time in many months. I found myself in a long valley with evergreens stretching up on both sides. I was walking through a meadow filled with sunlight, orange and yellow butterflies, golden sparrows, black-eyed Susans and daisies and their fresh smell in the breeze. A little brown-robed man shuffled and ambled beside me. And he told me about his Father and his Jesus and about God's wondrous love. Then I dreamed that invisible chains slipped from my spirit and rattled into a heap at my feet, and I worshiped my God as freely as this man Francis worshiped Him.

Chapter Fourteen

New Year's Eve

*"If truth be mighty, and God all powerful, His children need not
fear that disaster will follow freedom of thought,"*
Francois de Salignac de la Mothe Fénelon.

My first Christmas break in two years had turned into a
deprogramming, and my escape attempt out the bathroom
window had failed. If my next strategy didn't work, this would
probably be my *last* vacation as a member of the Unification
Church. The dread and queasy fear had left me. Like a front
line commando who becomes hardened to the idea of dying, I
had accepted the possibility of my own imminent spiritual
death. I would fight this one out to the end.

Even though the lights were blazing, the den seemed dark
and stuffy. Phil, Mom, Dad and Bruce sat in a circle around my
old sofa outpost. Three hours ago they'd foiled my bathroom
break, and after tempers had burst on both sides, everyone had
eventually cooled down to a more reasonable level of tension.

Earnest, sincere Phil sat on the edge of a kitchen chair
again, gesturing and rambling on about something in his
sensitive, soft-spoken manner. Vick and Sharon had left the
room for a while. I couldn't stand the sound of their voices
anymore and had stopped relating to them altogether. Phil I
could relate to, but Vick and Sharon had become too insanely
possessed by evil spirits.

My plan was nothing very original. Many Brothers and Sisters had already used it to escape *their* deprogrammers and
parents. Fake it. Go through the motions of "breaking." Pre-
tend that you realize that you've been deceived and brainwashed. Once they think you're deprogrammed, just wait for
the right time to spirit away.

I'm a terrible actor. So rather than acting out a dramatic realization scene that same day, I planned to break gradually over a two-day period.

After a few hours of obstinate debate I finally admitted to Phil that there was a small possibility that Sun Myung Moon was not the Messiah, just a slight one though. Then a few hours later I admitted that some of the Divine Principle's arguments and statements seemed shaky and might be "inaccurate." By this time Sharon and Vick had returned and seemed pleased by my "progress." And, oh yes, our fund-raising practices were not always the most legitimate. I told them that I felt badly about this. (I did feel badly; not because some of our selling tactics were morally wrong, but because they were absurdly bad PR.)

By 6:00 A.M. I'd created the impression that I was gradually coming around. Everyone started getting excited—they were swallowing it! At least 10 people had taken up their former positions in the den, except Dad, who sat on the floor with his arms locked around his jack-knifed knees. A little glint of hope flashed into his eyes. I had to look away.

Sharon had been fidgeting in her chair trying to let Phil do most of the talking. But my expression of doubts and reservations about the Unification Church was like the spring sun soaring into her six-month arctic winter. In a chirpy voice she burst in, "So, Steve! Do you think that Sun Myung Moon might not be the Messiah?"

I replied that I didn't know what to think anymore, that I was so confused, and yeah, I wasn't so sure that he was everything he claimed to be.

Then someone said that we'd made fantastic headway today and why don't we go to bed considering it's past six in the morning. Then Sharon jumped in her seat. "NO. If we stop now we'll have to start all over again tomorrow. Let's keep going."

In less than a minute Sharon had herded us into a circle and started into a short prayer. Then she asked me to pray. No turning back. I had to renounce Sun Myung Moon as my Messiah. I felt insulted and indignant that so many people opposed Father and the organization I'd devoted my life to. It didn't seem fair. On the other hand I felt like a slimy, chittering rat for conning everyone, especially Mom and Dad. I knew I would escape, nothing could stop me now, but this would tear them apart, devastate them. And they probably wouldn't see me again for several years. All these emotions converged and burst like a wave smashing on a sea wall.

I wept. And as I wept I apologized out loud to God for having followed a false Christ, a man who claimed to be His son but was in fact a fraud. "I'm sorry, God. I'm really sorry."

A beautiful ugly lie—combined with a very lucky but very spontaneous and authentic sobbing. And everyone fell for the show. Who wouldn't have?

Half the crowd was jumping up and down and clapping; the other half took turns holding me and squeezing me. Phil grabbed my hand and congratulated me on my new freedom. Vick, that obnoxious lovable guy, hugged me. Dad clutched my shoulders and kissed me. Then he held me at arm's length. When Dad is happy and looks at someone he loves, his eyes blaze like exploding, dancing, mirthful suns. No way I could look him square in the face. Then Vick shouted, "Let's go to Uncle John's Pancake House and celebrate!"

Everyone laughed, but the general consensus led us to bed and I slept miserably next to my loving Dad whom I wouldn't be seeing again for a long, long time.

Phil and Bruce would drive me around the East Coast on a rehabilitation program—three- or four-day visits with ex-Moonies and their families. After resting up for a day the three of us set off in the blue Volvo to visit Rabbi Davis in White Plains. He was a prominent religious leader and stood only a few notches below Ted Patrick in infamy as a diabolical anti-Moon and anti-cult activist. When someone said "Rabbi Davis" you thought of Satan.

My morale and faith in Father and the Family still ebbed at a frightening low. I had to break away before White Plains. Without a doubt, the influence of a man like Rabbi Davis would tip the scales of my teetering faith in, and allegiance to, the True Parents. I felt as weak and shaky as a bedridden stroke victim and it would only be a matter of time before I broke.

Phil spoke a great deal about thought reform, mind control and what I would be going through in the coming weeks. Although I wrote most of his explanations off as satanic mumbo-jumbo, with his degree in psychology and his commonsense approach he did have a good way of explaining these concepts.

He said his job as deprogrammer had been to provide the inconsistencies in Sun Myung Moon's ideology and group practices. This, he said, served to shock me—acted as a sort of irritant or stimulus, and forced me to take a closer look at the Unification Church and my commitment to it. "But," said Phil, "deprogramming is just one step towards completely breaking the control the Unification Church, or any cult, has over its members' minds." Of course my deprogramming had been the most important step. It had enabled me to start thinking for myself.

Phil made it clear that coming back into the outside world would be difficult. The road back to thinking rationally again was a long one. I would have to recover from the mental tyranny I'd been subjected to and from the disillusionment of having been deceived and exploited. So for awhile I would feel psychologically weak and confused, and might as well be prepared for "floating" experiences. Floating is the term used to describe the phenomenon of drifting back into the old cult thought patterns and states of mind. Yes, I would float, and perhaps even entertain the old delusions about Moon being the Messiah and begin to wonder whether leaving the Unification Church had been such a hot idea after all.

That's why the rehab program was so crucial. I needed support. Phil, the ex-Moonies and their families would help me talk out my experience and enable me to compare it with the cult experiences of other ex-members. In time I would become solid and strong again and understand more fully what had happened to me in the cult.

Yet they would not force any new values, beliefs or a new life-style upon me. And in the end, it would be up to me to reassess my experience and come to my own conclusions. Well anyway, that's what Phil talked about, and I listened alright. But it didn't make much of an impression. For the most part I believed that the whole field of psychology was ultra-humanistic and fallen.

We left Rochester in the late afternoon of December 31 and headed south on snow-patched highways, passing through bundled-up country towns. At every red light, at every restaurant or gas station stop I thought, *Should I break for it now?* But it always seemed too risky. Fortunately we never made White Plains and stayed the night in Phil's old student apartment in Binghamton.

I waited till Bruce and Phil were dead asleep. At 3:30 A.M. I slipped out of the building onto the icy sidewalk, fully equipped—long underwear, hat, gloves, and Tolkien's *The Hobbit*. From reading this inspiring book over the past two days I'd come to envision myself as the young Hobbit-hero escaping the dark powers of Mordor. Any second I expected Bruce or Phil to stick his head out the door. Then the chase would be on. I didn't feel fully consicous; it was more like a bad dream where you're being pursued but can't see where you're going or even know exactly what's chasing you.

Once I creaked over the frozen parking lot I heaved into a sprint and tore down the city street, past dark gas stations and stores. A few bars lined the street like colorful jukeboxes and poured out light, music and New Year laughter. Then I cut into the shadowy residential section and ran in the direction of the highway we'd come in on. I planned to cover as many miles as possible before daylight and then call headquarters to come pick me up.

Whenever car lights shot into my street I assumed that Bruce and Phil had found me. Then I'd plunge into a side street or across a snow-clogged backyard to lose them. Finally, I became so disoriented in the crisscross of city blocks that I had to ask for directions in a small hospital. I told the young middle-ager in the deserted waiting room that I was hitching back to Cornell University.

"Sure, that's up I-81. I'll give you a lift as soon as I give my aunt this mail."

He dropped me off at a rest area about two miles outside town. It was 5:00 A.M. and still dark. Hoping to get a ride to Cortland I canvassed the five or six cars parked around the bathroom facility. But the drivers were either local boys or starting off the New Year with their booze-flushed faces mashed into the car upholstery.

Then I called headquarters in New York from the phone booth in the parking lot, keeping an eye on the barren highway for cars. Cecil from Harry Porter's old team answered.

"Oh my God, Steve—there's no one here! They're all in Tar-rytown for God's Day."

Well, after that scare I called a half hour later and they'd found a leader, Mark Taine. "Yeah, Keith Karl's here with me. We're on our way." Just as daylight edged on the horizon I slid down a steep embankment and hid in the bushes along the river.

During the six hours before Keith showed I tramped circles on the snow in the sucking icy wind. But my body was warm with that victorious feeling. I'd given the agents of Satan the slip! Escaped spiritual death! With some cunning I'd fooled everyone, even Satan; fooled them all! Just for a few seconds a shadow flashed across my joy. This would be a black day for my family. I swept the thought away. That wasn't my fault. That was their tough luck for opposing the Messiah's Family.

It all came back to me during those first few hours with Keith and the God's Day celebration crowd—the reality of our restoration mission and my loyalty to it, my faith in Father. Keith and Mark had picked me up in a station wagon and we'd arrived at Belvedere just in time to see Father sing "Um Maya," one of his favorite Korean folk songs which we called "The River Song." The image of him as a coldhearted gruff man disinte-grated before the living figure of a dancing, smiling Sun Myung Moon. Any remaining fears or doubts I soon talked out with Keith.

The outdoor Belvedere stage opened into a huge tent pack-ed with Family members. Anyone from the East Coast MFT with a daily sales average over $150 had been allowed to attend the God's Day celebration. It was so good to be back in the Family. We sat on blankets to keep warm, drank pop, ate sand-wiches and potato chips, and watched Father hand out prizes to top fund-raisers—tapes of Divine Principle lectures, pictures of the True Parents. A few Sisters had even surpassed Father's standard of $400 a day and averaged over $500 a day during the Christmas rush. All day I milled around the tent and the various buildings on the estate talking to old buddies. I met old Oaklanders like Bento Leone and my own Arlane, IOWC friends like Werner and Isamu, old MFT mates and of course the high sellers on Justin's team. Theresa Baker was so glad to have me back she actually hugged me. Everyone had heard about my escape from the deprogrammers and I'd become a hero.

After I returned to my team in Richmond, Justin had me holy salt the clothes I'd taken from home and destroy the scarf Sharon had given me. These clothes probably still carried a number of evil spirits from the deprogramming.

That same week I made a special determination to become a rock-hard commando for the True Parents. I would study the *Divine Principle* and Father's words and brand them in my being. I would fight to develop a strong relationship with the Parents and ingrain in myself an unshakable loyalty to the Messiah and his bride.

I had always assumed that my faith in the True Parents was indestructible. Why should I be afraid of opposition and persecution, I thought, if I have the truth? But the deprogramming proved that even a person who solidly possesses God's highest truth can be forced to renounce it. Not only did I want to become a stronger member, I wanted to insure that any second deprogramming attempt would shatter in failure like a ship on the rocks.

A bitter angry month passed before I called my physical parents, and then only because Keith Karl told me to. That last week in January Mom had frantically assaulted the Unification headquarters with phone calls demanding to know if I'd ever returned. So I called her from a Newport News bowling alley one night.

"Oh, Stevie—we didn't know whether you went back or if you froze to death in some ditch." I was pretty cold to her and didn't try to hide the bitterness in my voice. Mom sounded sad and tired: no more wavy melody or cute yelping exclamations. "I hope we can still see you sometime," said Mom.

"No. I don't think so," my voice low-toned and flat. She asked if they might see me in a while after things cooled off. "I can't see you until you understand or at least accept what I'm doing . . . and I know that won't be for a long, long time." (I was thinking in the order of three to five years.)

That winter Bruce wrote me a letter. As I started into his clear, out-front style I suddenly heard his thoughtful voice speaking in my mind. The present—my Unification Church identity—melted away. And reality was whittled down to the two brothers who'd grown up together. Only a year apart, sometimes we'd been close, sometimes very distant. But I'd always fiercely respected Bruce and his judgment, his feeling for what made sense and what was complete rot.

"Stop being so pigheaded," Bruce was saying. The way I had cut myself off from my family was really hurting Mom and Dad: never writing, never calling, living so completely incognito that my parents had to funnel mail through Unification Church headquarters as if I were a POW behind the bamboo curtain. "You could at least write once in a while."

Then he completely sliced through my armor of resentment when he described how Dad wasn't the same since I'd returned to the Church. The spark had gone out of his eyes. He was quiet and moody under the weight of constantly worrying about me and the whole mess. And when Dad first found out that I'd taken off, his face had twisted into something horrible. His head drooping like a dying flower, he slowly climbed the stairs to the bedroom. Then the Kemperman children heard for the first time the uncontrollable weeping of their own father.

Chapter Fifteen

Three Years

*"But while he was yet at a distance,
his father saw him and had compassion,
and ran and embraced him
and kissed him,"
Luke 15:20.*

1976! The Year of great campaigns! Sun Myung Moon would speak out to America at two massive rallies—the "Bicentennial God Bless America Festival" on June 1 at New York's Yankee Stadium, and the Washington Monument rally on September 18 in the nation's capital.

Father wanted to pack Yankee Stadium to overflowing with 200,000 people. In his nine-city Day of Hope tour of Korea in 1975 sometimes as many as 100,000 people jostled outside listening to our leader's voice boom over the loudspeakers. Father hoped to reproduce that scenario at Yankee Stadium.

For me and for every member of the Unification Church, these two campaigns signified the dawn of national and world-wide acceptance. We believed these rallies would stem the tide of negative media publicity and show America that we were God's people, not a band of brainwashed religious fanatics. I even half-hoped that Mom and Dad would see the light.

Six weeks after my return from the deprogramming, Keith Karl transferred Justin's Virginia team back to Cleveland, piped in seven new fund-raisers and promoted me to the position of team leader. Fellow teammates had generally looked up to me as a "strong Brother" and good fund-raiser. And I guess my surviving the deprogramming had convinced Keith that I'd earned a crack at some leadership experience.

When Keith announced my new mission I felt suddenly unshackled and my heart whoopeed and whoopeed joy. After one-and-a-half years of tromping the streets in sun, cold and rain—no more fund-raising!

I soon tasted the wielding of the almost absolute power enjoyed by Church leaders. I was served first, I made all major decisions for my team; my orders could not be questioned.

Because of my new leadership position and my recent determination to implant myself in a rock-hard loyalty to the True Parents, I became more dedicated than I had ever been, a fighting, gung-ho follower of Sun Myung Moon. I allowed myself only three hours' sleep a night and worked hard at inspiring my team. Each morning before I dropped the team off we shrieked the Yankee Stadium motto till we were giddy, hoarse and punching the van's ceiling. "Go *Over!* Go *Over!* Go *Over!*"

> April, 1976
> . . . In my prayers . . . I tell God I would gladly die for
> victory in Yankee Stadium.

"If we fail in Yankee Stadium," said Regional Commander Karl, "we'll have to fight a World War III with real bloodshed [with the communists]. . . . So we must die for Yankee Stadium because if we fail now, we'll die later."

"Dying for Yankee Stadium" was one of the many inspirations which the leadership was diffusing around the movement. But for me, dying—dying for the cause, dying for the True Parents—took on powerful and mystical significance.

That spring I almost did die for the cause. Lack of sleep had dragged my body into spacey inattentiveness. One day I spaced right through a red light, exploded into a Vega, spun into a telephone pole and landed in a ditch—without a bruise fantastically enough. But Ma Bell did send me a bill for a new telephone pole.

The Family's driving record had to be the nation's worst! Brothers were forever falling asleep at the wheel. In 1976 we almost lost our insurance policy. I had brushed with Lady Death several times already when substituting for my team leaders. Once I woke up in the middle of a 60 m.p.h. death charge into a cement overpass piling—and swerved just in time. Some Brothers weren't so lucky. Jack Reagan had to be pried out of the wreckage after he fell asleep on a Baltimore bridge. Luckily, he'd suffered only a broken arm and a shattered jaw.

It was amazing how much Satan was working on all fronts to squash the Family. American newspapers were clogged with *nego* articles (negative, unfavorable to the group). The immigration authorities were deporting our admittedly illegal alien Japanese members. Of course our deprogramming buddies never slept. And we had IRS, FBI and senate investigations on our tail.

Sellers had to face a lot of negativity in the shops and parking lots. "Are you with Moon's group?" "Are you a Moonie?" Young members were often disturbed and shaken in their faith by this opposition or *persecution* as we called it. But with the older members, especially the stubborn ones like myself, the opposition only enraged us and boosted our allegiance to the underdog-Family.

Of all the struggles which confounded Family life, I only found one of them truly meaningful—my struggle to know God. Yet after all the trials and indemnity of the last two-and-a-half years I didn't feel much closer to God than when I'd first met the Family. Then one day I stumbled onto a touching parable and discovered God as if I'd never really known Him.

The Unification Church teaches that the evil spiritual world (and our own fallen nature) separates us from God—a God who grieves and weeps at the loss of His children and even bears resentment over the fall of man. By praying fervently, even pounding, shouting and screaming prayers, you can eventually pay enough indemnity to break through the evil spiritual world to God. When you begin crying and feeling "God's aching and grieving heart," you've broken through.

For two years I battled the denizens of the evil spiritual cloud bank, babbling and roaring my prayers during team prayer conditions, in the van, and into the lonely nights of campground forests and secluded city lots.

Sometimes I did break through to feel how much God probably grieved for and loved humanity. Occasionally, the feeling of having connected with God's heart seemed genuine. But so often it was like performing a technique and the resulting tears and emotions seemed contrived.

Of course I was more *conscious* of a God than two-and-a-half years ago. But all the work of screaming and fighting through a vast evil spirit world to reach our heavenly Father made Him seem very far away.

One night in February, I was holed up in the Cleveland Center's whitewashed prayer room perusing a Family booklet, *For God's Sake*. It was a unique and strongly Christian-flavored piece written by Miss Young Oon Kim. She'd taught New Testament studies at a Christian college in Korea before joining the movement. At one point I found myself engrossed in the New Testament story of the prodigal son.

I could visualize the father sitting on a porch, deep in sad thoughts about a long-lost son. Suddenly he spotted the boy approaching in the distance. The father didn't *wait* for the delinquent to come to him to beg for mercy, but took off running to *meet* his son. When he embraced his child he wasn't occupied with his son's terrible squandering and sinning. Rather, as if blinded by love, he thought only of his son's well-being—"This my son was dead, and is alive again; he was lost, and is found" (Luke 15:24)!

I couldn't believe it. Jesus' parable showed me in a few minutes what two-and-a-half years of search and struggle in the Messiah's family had *not* shown me—the all-embracing, beautifully-giving and unconditional nature of God's love. I felt suddenly filled with a comforting, glowing warmth that tingled from the crown of my head down to my feet. I began shedding tears of real joy as I realized that God lived inside me, that He'd been there all the time.

From that day on I stopped screaming my prayers like a hyena with stomach cramps and began talking softly with the God who lived inside. There was no need to shout. He wasn't lingering on the other side of an evil spiritual world *waiting* for my arrival. Rather, each time I came to Him in prayer, I knew He'd come rushing to meet me, and to embrace me in the warmth of His arms.

Two weeks before the Yankee Stadium Rally, Unification

Church members descended on New York City like the galloping hordes of Genghis Khan. We splattered posters of a smiling Sun Myung Moon across every unguarded patch of city. Brandishing tickets, we gaily chased down aloof sidewalking New Yorkers. The New Hope Singers and Go World Brass Band mobbed street corners and squares. By June 1 we'd distributed nearly three million free tickets. But a shadow flitted across our carnival spirits when a Japanese Brother was mugged during his nighttime door-to-door work and died two days later.

The Sunday before the rally, Father strutted back and forth across the outdoor stage at the Belvedere estate. The Sun Myung Moon who addressed a strict Family audience was shockingly different from the one I'd encountered at the Day of Hope talk in Berkeley. Amongst his followers he did not conceal his desire to influence and control world affairs. When he'd spoken to our MFT region in Washington, D.C. October 1975, he discussed the need to establish an international bank and control the world economy. "In fifteen years we must control all world affairs and set up the heavenly kingdom."[22]

Now, already tasting rally victory, he shouted, "There is no one in the world who will not hear the name of Reverend Moon . . ."[23] He explained that the time would come when rulers of the world, kings and queens, would ask us to come to their countries to influence their youth, their people.

Yankee Stadium looked dismally under-populated, and Father's five o'clock appearance was only an hour away. Then a 20-minute wind and rainstorm drenched the brass band, shredded banners and flattened our hot-air balloon.

At five o'clock Father began thundering from the red-carpeted platform. But throughout his delivery a distracting cacophony swept the bleachers—young street gangs ran wild and shouting, smoke bombs and litter pelted the crowd, pockets of protesters jeered and booed.

On June 2 the American Family flooded into Belvedere and our leader declared the rally a 100 percent victory. But a stooping malaise hung over the movement that day. We had worked so hard, and sacrificed and hoped so much to sway America. We'd expected a turnout of 200,000! And in the end we'd managed to muster only 25 or 30 thousand people. During the following days Japanese and American leaders chided us for gaining only a partial victory—our hearts hadn't been sincere, earnest and desperate enough.

I had many Brothers and Sisters in the Unification Church, but very few friends. The concept of friendship was somewhat foreign to our Brother-Sister style of relating (which did have its good points) and there was so little time for personal relationships.

Immediately after the post-rally mass workshop, I was appointed team leader under Mike Chapman. He turned out to be the friend I'd never had in the Unification Church. Our two-van team moseyed into my beloved West Virginia and together we worked nearly every workable background, "holler" and mountain town in the entire state. (We couldn't sell in the major cities of West Virginia because we'd been kicked out of most of them by 1976.)

During the summer mountain nights Mike and I sat in the van over cups of coffee or cider and discussed area and team problems. He was sensitive and easygoing, rare qualities among the disciplined Church leadership. And what a story that boy could tell! He had a sense of humor to rival Johnny Carson's. Sometimes we'd stay up into the wee hours laughing, joking and swapping tales. When we finally did part ways, I missed Mike, and I always remembered him as a rare and precious friend.

In September 1976, our West Virginia team drove up to D.C. for the six-million-dollar Washington Monument Rally: a monster rally complete with hired and Family entertainment, 1,600 chartered buses from six surrounding states, and a $100,000 gala fireworks display. This impressive publicity event attracted tens of thousands and blanketed the Washington Monument grounds.

Ten days after Washington Monument Keith Karl broke up our team and sent me to Louisville, Kentucky to be trained under a model Japanese leader, Isamu Kamyama. I would fund-raise, said Keith, and "inherit the 'Japanese standard' [Father's standard] and Isamu's great team-leading skills."

Gulp. Not fund-raising again! Selling in Louisville under

the Kamikaze Kamyama was like arriving in Dachau or Auschwitz after a Caribbean retreat. Although we raked in big money—myself $250-$325 per day, the Sisters $400-$500 per day, and the team $10,000-$13,000 per week—I found Kamyama's leadership harsh and unfeeling.

Throughout November and December, headquarters imposed several 21-day selling contests with hardly a breather between each competition. Kamyama allowed us three hours sleep per night and pitched us into 19- to 20-hour days during the advent of the coldest winter in Michigan history (10-15 degrees below). Every morning when he shook me awake, I shuddered at the sickening fatigue which still clung in my body, at the cold, empty and gruelling day ahead.

On Christmas day I wanted to phone my parents from our motel in Saginaw. But Isamu refused me permission, saying that I should have sent a card as my teammates had done. Finally, he gave in and I called home. (Some Japanese leaders had been known to prohibit members from attending their own parent's funerals, saying—"No! You are too important to mission!")

Mom sounded bright and pretty and Dad warm and happy. But then they asked if they could please visit me soon, and I became suspicious and hostile and began half-shouting that I didn't trust them, that I'd received "intuitions" that they were planning another kidnapping. (It turned out they had no such plans.) Mom started crying, "Stevie, it's been a year since we've seen you! I'm so afraid we'll never see you anymore."

My decision to stay underground was actually prompted by directions from headquarters. A rash of deprogrammings had struck. They'd even deprogrammed two high-level Oakland staff members whom I loved and respected: Evey Eden and Jacob Gadon.

It was January 1977. I stood at a fourth-floor bathroom window in the New Yorker Hotel and watched the snow fall on Eighth Avenue. Bundled figures padded the sidewalks. In spite of the three-day MFT workshop/vacation, I felt weighed down with disappointment and melancholy. After all the efforts of our two great campaigns, nothing seemed changed. The rallies had attracted only a handful of new members, and the opposition raged as ferociously as ever.

A few minutes before, I'd been milling in the lobby talking to old colleagues from my Oakland and early MFT days—Big Jim, Rosy Cottington, Rob Harten, Mike Tanner. I had known them when they were fairly young members, excited about the movement, hopeful and sparky. Now they looked out at me through sad, tired hound-dog eyes.

During those young-colt days all of us believed we'd be halfway to the kingdom of heaven by 1977! The entire Family did! Now in 1977 we simply *endured* our missions, like men chew dry, stringy meat.

As I watched from my window perch, a huge woman lumbered by down in the street, holding the hands of two tiny, skipping girls with candy-cane stocking caps. Their giggles drifted up through the falling snow. Then a strange thought flickered like an old lightbulb. I envied these people walking on Eighth Avenue. These folks had never heard the Messiah's calling. They weren't burdened with the responsibilities and pressures of our world-saving mission. They were free to saunter down Eighth Avenue and do as they pleased. No, they had never heard the Messiah's calling. And just for a few flickering moments, I wished I had never heard it either.

In mid-January Mom and Dad sent me a birthday card. I would be 22 years old in February. Mom wrote, "I hope and pray that you will call. As it is now, I cry every day. I don't understand how the Unification Church can be so cruel to parents."

After the workshop, I was back out fund-raising in the Youngstown-Akron area as a team assistant to Bob Marlin. We worked out of the new regional headquarters Keith had purchased—a comfortable rural home in the village of Hudson, Ohio. Every once in a while I asked Keith to make me a team leader. He said he would try, but explained that the MFT hadn't expanded since the campaigns were over.

One February night I took refuge in the prayer room. We'd trekked 12 hours of residential area in face-searing 13-below weather. I sat on my haunches and stared at the beige carpet, unable to shake a pattern of thought which was dragging me into a disillusionment and despair I had never known. After more than three years in the Unification Church, I was *still* fund-raising.

This realization had been flushed out by a blatant irony. I'd come to the Youngstown-Akron region at age 19 as a young-buck MFTer. Now, three years later, I was 22 years old and right back where I started from—in Youngstown-Akron fund-raising, fund-raising, fund-raising.

Then I remembered Daniel Silverman's words—"Why, in two years you'll be a world leader!" Of course I'd never taken his pronouncement literally, but I'd always expected to achieve a position of responsibility which would require and develop my talents and skills. Now, after three years, I realized I was the antithesis of a world leader—a 22-year-old peon-vender tramping through snowstorms and the coldest winter of his life.

I had personally raised over 100,000 tax-free dollars for my spiritual master. But I was developing no talents or skills, learning nothing. My heart and mind seemed stranded on a stale, joyless desert, like withered, dying cattle. And I'd lost nearly all hope for my personal future. When I looked into my future I saw myself trapped in a tunnel which lead to an ominous, dark wall.

Then suddenly something spoke to me from out of the past—"If you'd stayed in Berkeley you'd be graduating from college in two-and-a-half months." That was too much for me to handle. The "strong Brother," the unphaseable "slow thunder," as my teammates had nicknamed me, let his forehead sink to the carpet and his body heave with long, muffled sobs.

Every night during the past year I'd knelt on my sleeping bag and said my prayers before a small, framed color portrait of the True Parents. For over two years I had worked hard at developing a spiritual relationship with the Father and Mother of the universe, dedicating to them all my work, my financial gains, my prayers, my very life. Still, I continued to view Hak Ja Han as a mute little woman lost in a Messiah's shadow, and Sun Myung Moon as a tough-faced Oriental man—powerful, gruff, distant and aloof.

In recent months I'd asked other Brothers and Sisters about their relationship with the True Parents. To my surprise, many confided that they had trouble feeling close and relating to the Parents; in fact many had resigned themselves to side-stepping the Parents' mediatorship to relate directly to God.

One evening in late February I was in the prayer room reading Ken Sudo's *120-Day Training Manual*, the text for the former Barrytown missionary training program. I was completely absorbed in a sermon which included a discussion on the sacrificial example of Jesus Christ. Essentially, Sudo instructed us to follow Jesus' great example of love and sacrifice. From birth to death He had lived for all mankind.

That night, without even thinking or consciously deciding, I meditated on Jesus as I prayed. It was so *easy* to sense His warmth and compassion. In my mind's eye I could see His robed figure, the strong, clear eyes of understanding, the open hands which had healed, touched and comforted so many. He seemed like such an approachable man, someone you could talk to.

I recalled my experience with Father in 1975 when he spoke to our MFT region in the Washington Center's living room. I had wanted to give him a small, gift-wrapped box of chocolates which Lady Dr. Kim (Father's chief spiritualist) had personally holy salted. When he'd finished his delivery and started heading out of the room, I pressed the gift against his right hand and said, "Here, Father, for you."

Without flinching, or even looking aside, the glum-faced Father ignored my gift and bulldozed right past me into the dining room across the hall. So Sun Myung Moon remained for me an untouchable and distant man, a Messiah whom only the highest Church officials dared approach.

Not ever doubting our leader's messiahship, I continued to meditate on Jesus when I prayed. And doing this precipitated another breakthrough in my search for God. Jesus Christ's example as the Son of God helped me to grasp the nature of the often nebulous and hard-to-define heavenly Father. Like Son, like Father. I realized that the great tenderness and compassion of Jesus had found its origin in the tenderness and love of the Creator. What a breakthrough! Never had I felt so close to, so touched by my God.

Chapter Sixteen

Kidnapped!

"Oh, Lord, I want to be free, want to be free;
A rainbow round my shoulder, wings on my feet,"
Afro-American Spiritual.

On Saturday, April 2, 1977 I stalked potential candy buyers
in a Massillon, Ohio shopping center. The rain fell in misty
curtains until my hair dripped stringy and my clothes stuck to
my body.

By 5:30 P.M. the parking lot had almost completely emptied.
The rain had stopped half an hour before. I noticed a small
cluster of people milling around a turquoise Dodge family van. I
trotted up to the driver's window, smiled and pointed to my
candy. A balding gentleman and his wife smiled back and
shook their heads. Then they motioned towards the rear of the
van where a tall young guy with a mane of long blond hair was
toting a grocery bag and chatting with a mustachioed friend.

I asked the blond guy if he would buy some candy to help our
"Christian youth centers."

"Yeah, sure. Let me get my wallet." He swung the back door
open and set his groceries down. A long-haired kid was sitting
against the van wall smoking a cigarette, his face buried behind a *MAD* magazine. Then the big guy said, "OK, let's *DO IT!*"
and simultaneously rammed into my tail end and sent me
hurtling into the van. The kid with the *MAD* magazine grabbed
me from behind and began dragging me to the floor.

My first thoughts were, *They want my money.* No fear.
Just cold anticipation. I expected them to slit my throat, and I

was ready to die for God and the True Parents. A second later my mother—my own mother—popped up from behind the back seat, looking very frightened. I tore loose and spun around to face my brother Bruce. Then I thought, *Oh God— deprogramming!*

In that moment I nearly blacked out under the most horrible fear I had ever known. I didn't care if thieves slit my throat, but this Satan-possessed family of mine had returned to destroy my spiritual life, to kill me for all time!

I began screaming for help and dove for the open door. Bruce tackled me. With my arms wrapped around the bumper, the thugs outside struggled to close the door while inside pairs of strong male arms worked to pry me loose.

In horror, like a man watches his fingers give out on the cliff's edge, I felt my grip tire and my body being sucked into the van. The door slammed and the van gunned out of the parking lot. Squirming under Bruce and the blond dude, I felt handcuffs click around one wrist. When they bound my feet I stopped fighting and lay breathing hard on the carpeted floor.

With my mother caressing my head and trying to comfort me, I scrunched my eyes shut and began to silently chant. I decided to mentally recite the entire *Divine Principle* from first to last lecture. I would not be turned against the truth, against the True Parents. Never. Never. I vowed to die first before they broke me.

The van turned down a dirt road where they carried me to a windowless U-Haul van. In the darkness I heard an older man's earnest voice telling them to be careful. Not until minutes later did I realize it was my father.

As the van raced through the Ohio night I peered at the circle of white, tense faces. Nervous comments. The Dutch couple up front kept barking orders. Satan. The van tasted and stank of Satan.

Hours—hideous hours later they pulled into a driveway, then lugged me towards a mansion-house. In the moonlight it loomed huge and sinister like a witch's castle. Now was my chance! I spit the loose gag out of my mouth and let hot, curdling screams shatter the night quiet. Panic! Jabbering and yelling. Then Bruce shoved a T-shirt in my mouth and told me to shut up. Breathing wildly through my nostrils I was rushed to an upstairs bedroom and eased onto the bed.

The next morning three deprogrammers arrived at the witch's castle—the stately Rochester home of Mr. and Mrs. Trommel—the Dutch couple who'd piloted the vans. I sat on the bed vacillating between numbing shock and a certain confidence that I could escape back to the Family as I had before.

As the deprogrammers talked, I fought to shut out their Satan-inspired lies and stay "connected." I mentally chanted and envisioned the smiling faces of True Mother and Father. Sometimes these techniques were so successful that my mind drifted into a twilight sea of Family faces and conversation, leaving the earnest voices of the deprogrammers far behind, like the murmurings of children on a distant shore.

For four days I refused to speak. At the end of the fourth day the Human Wall decided to fake it. I knew I could fool them again because no one had ever found out that I'd faked my last deprogramming in 1975. So I started to talk, and led everyone on until one of the deprogrammers asked, "So who do you think Sun Myung Moon is?"

With my head in my hands and in a voice of confusion I replied, "I don't know, I just don't know, but he's *not* the Messiah!"

Everyone seemed to fall for it; and a general spirit of jubilation filled the house which by now was overrun with old Bastian Road and family friends. And just after I "broke" a well-known deprogrammer arrived, Steve Hassan. From the moment he opened his mouth I was glad I'd faked it when I did. I wouldn't have enjoyed trying to spiritually and mentally fend off a long session with this articulate fellow and his mounds of tapes, notes and documents. He'd worked as a *Divine Principle* lecturer and had personally known Father and many top leaders. His inside knowledge of the Family was phenomenal.

Then who of all people should call up, but dear Barb Underwood, a favorite Oakland Sister. She had just been deprogrammed through the landmark custody case in San Francisco which granted 30-day conservatorships to five sets of parents over their "Moonie-children."

Through Barb we also learned of the attempted kidnapping of a daughter of a prominent Bay area woman. In front of her own mother the Oakland Sister had slashed her wrists with a razor. She was rushed to the hospital and there reclaimed by the Oakland Family.

"Good for her!" I thought.

Of course Mom and Dad were rejoicing over my "successful deprogramming." But I didn't feel like a heel for conning them as I had at the last deprogramming. I'd had well over a year to brand in myself an unwavering loyalty to the True Parents, which by now was icier and more merciless than ever. In reaction to all my parents' sincere efforts I felt only mean, resentful deadness. They would just have to accept my allegiance to the Family.

Meanwhile, I calculated; plotted my escape. I got scared for a moment when Hubert called from home and suspected that I was far from deprogrammed. "Are you sure you're alright, Steve? You're still talking with that dead monotone."

The next morning Dad announced they were driving me to a rehabilitation center for ex-cult members in New Hampshire. Steve Hassan, Bruce and Hubert would accompany us. Since they were watching me so closely, I decided to postpone my escape attempt until an opportune night at the rehab center.

Chapter Seventeen

Carriage House

"Great is truth, and it prevaileth,"
I Esdras iv, 41, the Apocrypha.

Patches of snow dabbled the barren mountains and winding roads as our Chevy climbed through Vermont into New Hampshire. In the hamlet of Claremont, a gnarled board sign pointed us to Chelsey where the rehabilitation center bordered a small lake. The rehab center, a rustic 150-year-old carriage house, was the summer home of the program's directors—Dr. and Mrs. George Swope.

The Swopes had lived out their own successful rescue and deprogramming saga a couple years back with a Family member who became involved in the Unification Church. Mrs. Swope is a nurse-teacher at the Midland School in Rye, New York. Dr. Swope, an ordained American Baptist minister, is in the department of counseling and student development, and adjunct professor of psychology at Westchester Community College in Valhalla, New York.

Steve Hassan had already described the four-week rehab program—it had nothing to do with deprogramming, and everyone participated of his own free will. If at any time a "rehabber" wanted out, the parents were called to come pick her/him up. On Saturday and Sunday Dr. Swope held study sessions on the Bible and the psychology of cult membership; during the week the Swopes worked in New York while the Carriage House folks enjoyed a lot of free time.

In the gentle gloaming of early spring, the Carriage House

looked harmless and peaceful. But when the six of us filed into the cavernous living room, I swamped in panic and began praying and chanting wildly to myself—"Heavenly Father! Help me get out of this satanic place!" I felt trapped in the bowels of the anti-cult movement, an evil fraternity bent on destroying our spiritual family. I hated these people more than anything on earth. Trapped in Satan's den! I fought to keep from ripping the door open and plunging into the mountain night.

Joy Shores, the blonde-banged and bespectacled head of staff, greeted us with a pleasant North Carolina drawl and also introduced a few staff people and rehabbers. Everyone except Joy was a former member of some religious cult—Hare Krishna, Children of God, The Way, Body of Christ, The Forever Family (also Church of Bible Understanding). Gradually I calmed down and began milling around the room, perceiving it as a viperous medieval dungeon.

A wood stove crackled its warmth and gave out the aroma of burning pine. Huge vinyl "bean bags" lounged near the fire like voluptuous toadstools. A massive bookcase lined the wall opposite the door. And from the walls and ceiling hung an array of antiques—wagon wheels, lamps, wooden buckets, and yokes.

In the middle of all the shuffle and buzz Mom introduced me to a distinguished-looking man, white-haired and mustachioed. I'd pictured Dr. Swope as something possessed and sinister. But here he was, shaking my hand in a warm welcome and asking if I wanted some dinner. He had a chuckling, eloquent way about him, like a charming, witty professor.

On this particular Sunday evening, Dr. Swope conducted a Bible study on Isaiah; at 9:00 P.M. he and his wife set off on the five-hour return trip to their home in suburban New York.

Around midnight, staff and rehabbers climbed into the newly constructed loft bedrooms above the living room—women in the north room, men in the south room. But my escape plan crumbled like a madman's dream. There was a 30-foot drop from the loft window, and ex-Moonie staff member Jim Hadley slept with his bed on the trap door. Well, back to the old escape-out-the-bathroom-window method.

The next morning Mom and Dad left. A little before sack-out time that night I was already locked in the bathroom; the shower drowning out my fierce, mumbled prayer for deliverance from Satan's rehab center. My throat felt taut and thick as I heaved up on the window. It opened several inches then jammed against something. Oh Moses—wooden blocks screwed into the window frame! For a moment I considered postponing this getaway until I'd removed or loosened the blocks. *No!* I thought, *You've got to get away! Now!* I ripped off my cowhide coat, shoved my head and shoulders through the narrow opening and squirmed hard. But my thick, leather belt caught on the window's edge and refused to budge.

Just then someone lifted the shades of a window across the yard and saw me half-dangling out the window like a weasel in a trap. It was Rick Lorie, a new ex-Moonie rehabber. Then there was shouting and stomping and seconds later Rick stood pleading at the door, while six-feet-four-inch ex-Krishna staff person named Andy Sharples towered outside in the yard. I teetered on the bathroom floor; shaking, sweating and think-ing—*Oh, God, I blew it! Who knows when I'll get another chance?! Oh, God, I blew it.*

To my surprise, everyone was very kind and understanding about the episode. I lied that I'd been frightened by a "vision of Moon" so they'd think I was "floating" rather than quite unde-programmed.

The following afternoon the dozen or so rehabbers and staff people were sunbathing along the mill stream which flowed from the lake to the mill dam. I was leafing a book, judging my chances of being able to sprint around the house and into the woods. Then, my shock-for-the-day bounced around the corner of the house and hugged me. It was my mother, my mom. Of course she'd heard about my attempted escape and gunned it all the way from Rochester. She was going to stay for a week.

That night she asked me to stop by at the guest bedroom to say goodnight. We sat on the bed and talked some and then she held me in her arms and asked, "Are you really alright, Stevie? Are you really alright?"

And I just stared at the wall and thought, "My poor, poor lovesick mother. My poor lovesick mother."

But as I lay in my attic bed that night, smelling the room's freshly cut pineboards, something stirred inside me—one gear in a system that had gone dead and rusted over. I felt a grain of pity or sorrow for my mom, a ghost of an ancient but once very great love. I couldn't bear to take off while Mom was around. In my mind I could already see her weeping and gasping in horror as a mother saw her son disappear forever into a world she had come to know and fear—"the cult," terrible prison of young hearts and minds. That night I decided, like a coward, to put off any escape attempts until after Mom had left.

In the following days I got more details on the purpose of the Carriage House. The program was designed as a four-week period where ex-cult members voluntarily could examine their respective religious cult from a point of view outside the group, free from its pressures and influences. It was a time of readjustment to the outside world, an opportunity to make a more objective evaluation of the group.

There were good reasons for the blocked windows and Jim Hadley on the trap door at night. The first reason was to keep the cults *out*. Hare Krishna, for instance, had been known to surround the homes of ex-cult members and chant loudly to retrieve them. (In the Family, top leaders such as Keith Karl sometimes spent entire days in track-down rescue attempts of defecting and deprogrammed members.) The second reason concerned the need to restrain ex-cult members, who being initially confused and psychologically weak, are prone to floating and sudden impulses to return to the cult.

Dr. Swope explained that the rehab program practiced restraint, *not* incarceration. Rehabbers frequented restaurants, movie theaters, musical performances and nearby ski slopes and had plenty of opportunity to run off if they were set on returning to the cult. "Your parents aren't asking much of you," explained Dr. Swope, "just four weeks to examine an organization which is demanding a total life commitment."

I had to take my hat off to the incredibly positive, relaxing and vibrant atmosphere at the Carriage House. While the stereo filled the living room with popular, folk, rock, and Christian music, we lounged at the table or plopped in bean bags—reading, playing backgammon and chess, doing macramé. I didn't talk much, but enjoyed overhearing *non ex-Moonie* rehabbers and staffers relate their incredible cult experiences.

Sometimes we took walks in the country, canoed, fished, or enjoyed events like Mose Allison's jazz trio.

In the beginning I viewed myself strictly as an infiltrator gathering intelligence. But I soon began relishing the Carriage House program as a post-combat G.I. relishes a long overdue vacation. OH! After all that fund-raising, the *joy* of curling up in a bean bag near the wood fire and doing absolutely nothing! For me, "nothing" meant devouring novels and philosophical texts, looking up to the clouds creeping across the mountains, gazing into the enchantment of red, glimmering coals and then returning to my precious books. After three years of non-scholastic, round-the-clock labor, my hunger for learning burned like a field of dry goldenrod.

Yet much of the time I drifted in and out of paranoia and bitter detachment, obsessed with wild escape plans. Every morning when I woke to find myself in the rehab house I'd think, *What am I doing here!? . . . Why don't I get out? God doesn't want me here!* Then nausea, fear and guilt would flood the pit of my stomach.

I was still a Unification Church member; and to remain strong and connected, I stood under chilling "indemnity showers" and prayed desperately in the bathroom two or three times a day. Yet I'd never felt so weak and run-down. I ate like a starving jackal, and slept ten hours a night.

One evening, about a week later, the Carriage House gang took a saunter around the lake. The sun was settling behind shadowy mountains and wispy streamer-clouds of purple, blue and tinted rose. Nancy Smith, ex-Children of God member and staff person, sat on my shoulders and yelped and giggled every time I charged ahead through the warm night.

When we all reached the bridge at the stream/lake junction, I strode along the bridge's edge and suddenly pretended to lose my footing—Nancy screamed. I laughed and laughed and it felt so good. Joy Shores chuckled, "I can't believe it! Is this the zonked-out guy with the crazy stare who stumbled into the Carriage House last week?"

"And he's *talking*!" said Nancy, who'd vise-gripped my head so I couldn't throw her in the lake as I'd done earlier.

It was true. I was talking, enjoying myself, opening up, and—*thinking*. Yes, I was doing a lot of thinking. Dr. and Mrs. Swope amazed me! People in the fallen world weren't supposed to be so highly moral, so deeply caring and serving. When their lovely old, brown Buick rolled into the driveway Friday night, it was like "Moms" and "Pops" coming back to the ranch—cheers and hugs, Mrs. Swope herding us around the living room table, stacks of brownies and hot chocolate, rolling-crashing-rolling waves of conversation and a surprising feeling of being "home."

Mrs. Swope breathed heartiness and motherly concern, Dr. Swope great humor and wise anecdotes. And though I still opposed the Swopes' anti-cult efforts, I now admired them for sticking their necks out to help the young victims of religious cults. In fact Hare Krishna was already harassing the Swopes and Joy Shores with a $1,000,000 lawsuit. My own Unification Church was suing Dr. Swope for $9,000,000.

But more than anything else, I realized that Dr. and Mrs. Swope were a living testimony that a person could, in the world outside the Unification Church, love God deeply and live full lives of faith, sacrifice and devotion.

The kindness and charm of the resident females also worked powerfully on this combat-worn soldier of the True Parents. In the Family I'd learned to cut off or stifle any feelings of attraction for women because they were "Adam and Eve problems," inspired by Satan. Physical contact between men and women was absolutely taboo (Onni's Oakland Center was a frowned-upon exception to this rule).

Perhaps my defenses were down because I often caught myself staring helplessly at the women. Caroline Bowles, a staff person who'd spent five terrible years in the "Body of Christ," would sometimes get concerned about my troubled looks and sit down to talk with me. I couldn't remember having met a sweeter person. And those blue eyes and flowing hair the color of a wheat field browned in the sun—I'd start to gawk and forget where I was. Occasionally, I would catch myself, *Whoa! This is the work of "old Snake Face!"* But these defenses usually lasted about 2.5 seconds. Emotions which had been dead for years were coming back to life.

And then one afternoon I was lying facedown on my bed, wallowing in confusion and nausea and perhaps a certain amount of self-pity. Then a James Taylor song with its soothing guitar work rose up through the loft floorboards—"Shower the People."

Something shuddered deep inside me, like a plucked string of a bittersweet cello. I felt shamed by the Christian example of the Swopes and the staff and realized how cold and unloving I'd been towards my loving parents and family.

Then I began to wonder about my spiritual growth during the last three-and-a-half years. But I got scared and smothered the thought, afraid that a close self-examination might prove I'd advanced little (or even lost ground) towards my original goal of becoming a more giving, more loving person.

One more thing which deeply impressed me in the course of the week were Dr. Swope's study sessions on the Bible. In the Unification Church the Bible is, practically speaking, considered a dead book which has been superseded by the "Completed Testament," i.e., the *Divine Principle.*

During one Saturday session Dr. Swope issued a compelling exhortation. "If the Unification Church is going to base its 'Divine Principle' ideology almost entirely on the Bible [which it does], then I think Unification members should at least make a genuine effort to *understand* what the Bible says!"

I soon took up the Reverend's "challenge" and began poring through the Bible, not so much to see if the *Divine Principle* contradicted the Bible (Dr. Swope's main argument for why Unification members should investigate it), but because the clergyman had helped me discover surprising richness and depth in the ancient book. It was like stumbling onto a dusty manuscript in a dark cave and realizing, as my flashlight beamed the brittle pages, that I'd discovered a 5,000-year-old record of the history of God!

These encounters with the Bible and the living Christianity of the Swopes had finally left me hanging with one thrilling/disturbing hunch—perhaps God was not just working in the Unification Church. Perhaps the heavenly Father could be found elsewhere.

The experiences of that week carried me to the brink of a surprising realization—a realization which caused me to begin opening up to long lost parts of myself and to the world around me.

The day Mom left the Carriage House I was holed up in my bathroom prayer-booth suddenly realizing what I, a die-hard follower of Sun Myung Moon, *never* believed I would *ever* realize—the full and awful significance of a lifelong commitment to the Unification Church. We weren't talking about a summer at Camp Granada. No. Rather, my *life* was at stake! My God-given life on this earth! Then I thought, *Holy cow, I'd better be sure the Family is really what I think it is!*

It was then that I more or less decided to stick out the rehab program. I would do my best to listen to and deal with the arguments of the anti-cult movement. And if after listening to these arguments I could refute them and prove to myself that the Unification Church was true, then I felt I could in good conscience return to the Family.

My new strategy included an admission that there was probably some truth to the current theories of mind control as expounded by certain psychologists and psychiatrists. One such theory holds that exposing a person who has recently left a religious cult to stimuli such as cult reading material, lecture tapes and cult songs, tends to reinstate and/or reinforce cultic perceptions and states of mind.

I had to admit that this theory might be more true than not. And I wanted to be as objective as possible in my examination of the anti-cult point of view. So I stopped humming Family songs, decided not to read the *Divine Principle* book and "Master Speaks" which I'd "found" in the Swopes' bedroom, and instead of praying "in the name of the True Parents" I started praying "in the name of our loving God" or "in Jesus' name." Here I reasoned that since Jesus was supposed to be rallying behind our movement, directing my prayers through Him would guarantee one of two results—if the Unification Church was the true way Jesus would guide me back *into* the movement; if it was a false way He'd guide me *out*.

Though I was sure I would never leave the Family, I *guiltlessly* struck upon this plan of action. For it flowed out of a genuine desire to pursue what was right and true. I realized that my belief in the movement had to be founded in clear conscience and pure conviction, not in self-indoctrination and avoidance of threatening counter arguments.

And I struck upon this strategy *joyfully* because I was in no hurry to scuttle back to the life of fund-raising I hated so bitterly.

Chapter Eighteen

Revelation

"The biggest disease today is not leprosy or tuberculosis, but rather the feeling of being unwanted, uncared for and deserted by everybody. The greatest evil is the lack of love and charity, the terrible indifference towards one's neighbor who lives at the roadside assaulted by exploitation, poverty and disease,"
Mother Teresa of Calcutta.[24]

The following weeks at the Carriage House passed in and out of a tortuous limbo, a tug-of-war between the Unification Church and the outside world: half-hell/half-heaven.

Every morning I woke to the same fear-full, guilt-full nausea—*Am I deserting God's true family? What's happening to me?* And when Dr. Swope's or staffers' criticism of the Church seemed too sharp, I often closed up like a clam and steamed for angry hours—sometimes retaliating into thoughts of bolting into the mountains to get away from everyone. All this was sheer hell.

On the other hand, the free time and the wonderful experiences we rehabbers shared were absolute heaven—pillow fights, dancing to records, sliding down the trap door ladder on our mattresses, picnics, swimming and swamping the canoe, diving off the bridge, cramming into our three cars and roaring off to the bowling alleys, drive-in movies and ice cream parlors.

With almost every experience I realized, "Wow! This is the first time I've done this in *years!*" And then the old feeling of being young, wild and *alive* would wash over me like a crashing beach-wave and leave me laughing and tingling.

In the course of this tug-of-war between two worlds, I began experiencing gradual shifts in the way I perceived the Unification Church. Perhaps these shifts were caused by my recent disillusionments about the movement. Actually, they were *old* disillusionments that I'd managed to repress or deftly rationalize away. Now the input of the rehab program was causing them to surface like bloated cadavers. There was my long-time resentment that I'd been robbed of a college education. I also felt the ghost of past shame for having supported Nixon during our ludicrous Watergate rallies.

Then my old fears and mixed feelings about Sun Myung Moon's matchmaking came bobbing to the surface. I'd always sensed that the relationships of "blessed couples" were unusually lacking in real warmth and fulfillment. And I could never forget how my former team captain, Justin Kleinman, had gone off to Korea to be "blessed" in the mass wedding of 1,800 couples in 1975. Sun Myung Moon had matched him with a woman he'd met only once before, and the day after their brief honeymoon in Seoul his bride was shipped off to missionary work in East Africa. Not only were couples often split up, but their children were usually cared for by the Barrytown nursery. Several times "the blessing" had struck close to home in the form of terrible visions of being paired up with a 300-pound Sister.

One after the other, three-and-a-half years of doubt and repressed disillusionment began to break loose. And with my first major shift in perception, the Unification Church began to appear unnaturally restricting, much too controlled and stern in its life-style.

Then one morning, three weeks into the Carriage House program, I suddenly perceived Sun Myung Moon as an ordinary man running a mass movement. It was immediately clear that I'd turned down a path which led right out of the Unification Church. From that day on the great fear of possibly rejecting God's true Messiah haunted me like a swooping carrion bird.

Several times a week, my bathroom prayer-times degenerated into bouts of weeping and wrestling with this fear: "What if I leave the movement and it turns out that Sun Myung Moon *is* God's true son. Then for the rest of *eternity* I will be branded with the stigma of having rejected the Messiah."

At one point, in my desperation to be free of this agony, I did consider suicide. I reasoned that once I entered the spirit world I would immediately find out whether or not Mr. Moon was our man; for the billions of the good spirit world were supposed to be mobilizing behind the true Messiah-king. But suicide! The fear and the turmoil had actually driven me to consider suicide. And then I finally understood why so many ex-cult members had ended up in psychiatric wards.

Yet there was something powerful at work which would often drive away my fear of possibly rejecting the true Messiah, and make this fear seem without basis—my growing fascination with the Christian faith.

After my first week at the Carriage House I spent many hours each day in my bean-bag-perch consuming theological texts, books by Christian writers such as C. S. Lewis, books on biblical exegesis, and the Bible itself. At times I found myself peering down the corridor of time and wishing I could question all the great men who'd been inspired and changed by the message of Christ—Albert Schweitzer, Martin Luther, Thomas Aquinas, Augustine, Paul of Tarsus. Had they felt what I was feeling now? That here was an idea that made sense and left your soul enriched and inspired about life?

I found the Bible so rich with God and history that I could envision Jeremiah preaching in the marketplaces, Isaiah's great vision in the Temple, Jesus weeping at the tomb of Lazarus. Though I tended to believe in the main tenets of the *Divine Principle,* the message of Sun Myung Moon, compared to the message of Jesus, seemed empty, sterile and eclectic, like a heap of unrelated chemistry formulas.

Dr. Swope commented at one study session that "a religious organization which does nothing for the benefit of people outside the group should be viewed with suspicion." (This being one possible criterion for distinguishing cults from true religious endeavors.) I had winced, remembering how much it had always bothered me that the Unification Church did nothing for outsiders. I had always hoped that my work in the movement would help make some improvements in the world; yet all we ever did was recruit and fund-raise. All our projects were directed towards the immediate expansion of the organization. Even our brief campaign to clean up the sidewalks and streets of New York had been a publicity stunt for Yankee Stadium. It appeared that the Unification Church didn't give unless there was something to be received.

I wondered if Christianity could inspire true selfless giving. In my search for an answer to this question I was attracted to a book about Mother Teresa of Calcutta—*Something Beautiful for God*, by Malcolm Muggeridge. It turned out that this lone Catholic sister has put the entire Unification Church to shame with her work in the slums of Calcutta, establishing schools, hospitals and a home for dying destitutes.

Mother Teresa's daily prayer wasn't, "Lord, help me fund-raise!" but rather, "Dearest Lord, may I see you today and every day in the person of your sick, and whilst nursing them, minister unto you."[25] She constantly reminds us of Jesus' words—"I was hungry and you gave me food, I was thirsty and you gave me drink . . . as you did it to one of the least of these my brothers, you did it to me" (Matt. 25:35,40).

One Sunday morning the Swopes and a few Carriage Housers visited the American Baptist Church in Newport. A tethered pig and goat were munching on the front lawn when we pulled in. Dr. Swope explained, "The church is trying to raise funds to purchase livestock for an East African village."

Well, I thought, *at least they're not all hot air. They're doing something.*

It was a friendly, intimate church where the robust minister could boom, "Good morning!" and the congregation chuckle to a good witticism. Throughout the service I couldn't shake the impression that I'd stumbled upon the New England descendents of the Pilgrims, of the folk who'd fled here to worship their God freely. It seemed their joy and devotion hadn't changed much in the last three centuries. A golden, bright spirit flowed in the church, a warm feeling of worshiping together. I sensed that God lived here in this little church, in these people—a feeling I'd seldom experienced in all my Family Pledge and Prayer services.

And just as I'd envied Saint Francis, I envied these New

Hampshirites for the way they freely and independently related with their God. My own relationship with God had long seemed entangled in the endless demands and politics of our world-saving mission. So often I'd felt like a nameless pawn in the hordes of a movement bent on spiritually conquering the world—driven to exhaustion, left with little time to pursue a personal spiritual life. What little prayer time we did have was often railroaded into requests for victory in our restoration mission. It was becoming a conscious hope—that I might someday realize a no-strings-attached relationship with the heavenly Father.

It was early evening and I lay sprawled on my back in a bean bag. Nancy and Donna were guitaring and singing on a nearby bench. Then they started into, "Come to the Water," mellow and gentle.

> Come to the water, stand by my side.
> I know you are thirsty, you won't be denied.
> I felt every teardrop when in darkness you cried.
> And I strove to remind you
>   that for those tears I died.[26]

Suddenly a feeling of standing next to a living Jesus overwhelmed me—intense warmth, tenderness. I dropped my book in my lap and closed my eyes. Seconds later I felt completely embraced in acceptance. *Acceptance!* I couldn't believe it. How different from the distance and fear I always felt for the Korean Messiah. But what did it mean? Was Jesus showing me the way back *in* or *out* of the movement? I just didn't know.

In any case, I felt strongly that I had been given a sign that everything was going to be all right. And the comforting feeling was so wonderful that it swelled into silent tears.

My admiration and love for the founder of Christianity grew stronger in time. I began to wonder *why* after several years of praying "in the name of the True Parents" and dedicating my *entire life* to Sun Myung Moon and his wife did I feel almost no love for and from them as compared to an overwhelming love for and from Jesus Christ?

During my fifth and last week at the Carriage House it struck me that the world looked a whole lot different than it had five weeks ago. I now realized that there was a 50-50 chance that the Unification Church was dead wrong, merely a counterfeit messianic movement, and that I could possibly begin a new life in the vast, alluring outside world.

I started watching dear old Walter Cronkite with the 6:30 world news—international diplomacy, the American family, the economy—a vibrant world with real problems, real triumphs and real people. For the first time I felt like a participant in a world community rather than a contemptuous, self-righteous outsider, as I had been for three-and-a-half years.

In the Family I'd held a god's-eye view of a wasteland world infested with evil, with people who were spiritually dead, empty and wandering in grey depression. This dark world view had even reshaped and distorted the memory of my earlier life. But now old Bob Dylan and Beatle records were triggering heart-warming memories of days in high school and Europe.

And there was this one song which Caroline and an ex-Moonie staffer named Terry were fond of singing. No matter what state I was in, whenever Caroline's soft, sweet voice and Terry's guitar chimed forth this pretty song I was always moved: "Find that light in the depth of your darkness . . . O, let it shine. Let it shine, shine on."[27] Then shudders of hope—of bubbling, fiery hope—would race through my body. And a great red sun would burst over a new horizon which had squeezed into my life—a great warming light that pierced the deadness, that burned off the oppressive fog to expose a pure, magnificent landscape. Then I would daydream of a new life in a new world—my own place to live, my own personal friends, camping trips, a girlfriend to talk to and be close to, back to college. And most especially, I could seek God freely, as I saw fit, and with *joy*. Could it ever be? I prayed that God would show me His way, "Please, Father, I have to know, I must know."

That week I decided to live out one last journey. By this time I was fed up with everybody! With both the Unification Church and with the opposition movement. I felt the need to continue my search and investigation in a completely neutral environment. As soon as possible, I would set off to travel, read, think and pray to determine whether I would return to the Unification Church or break with it, finally and forever.

Chapter Nineteen

The Last Journey

"And Freedom rear'd in that August
sunrise Her beautiful bold brow,"
Alfred Tennyson.

In mid-May I visited Mom and Dad for a short week then returned to stay at the Carriage House until the end of June. I was still trying to prove to myself the veracity of the "Divine Principle" and the Unification Church in the face of the many counter arguments. But I had also started compiling a list of disturbing discrepancies and shortcomings I was now noticing in Church ideology, policy and practice. If and when I returned to the group I would pose my list of questions to Mr. Salonen and other top leaders.

During this time I also decided to seek out a friend I'd known in the movement whom I highly respected and who'd come out by himself—Gary Johnson. I *had* to talk to a former member who'd come out of the Unification Church on his own. I just couldn't believe the testimony of *deprogrammed* ex-Moonies because I'd learned that *they*, not Unification Church members, were the actual victims of brainwashing and deception. My final decision as to whether or not to return to the

Unification Church would depend on what I learned from Gary—how he was doing, his reasons for leaving the group.

From the end of June, I spent six weeks with my folks in Rochester before I took off on my spiritual sojourn. At home, without the wonderful atmosphere and distractions of the Carriage House, the haunting fear of rejecting a possibly true Messiah had returned in full force and plunged me into an agonizing limbo. I prepared for my trip, earning some money and assembling gear. But I kept postponing my departure until "tomorrow."

On Thursday, August 11 the Kemperman family began the drive to Austin. The University of Texas had invited Dad to come down for a year (1977-78) as a visiting professor. Then around 4:00 in the morning of August 15, I slipped out of our motel room in Little Rock, Arkansas, leaving a small diary explaining my reasons for leaving. Toronto, Canada was my ultimate destination.

Just the experience of getting out in the world and talking with all kinds of people felt natural and good and started opening things up for me, a babe's eyes opening to a new and beautiful world, to ever-changing places and people. And what precious people! I met tobacco-chewing Arkansas farmers, a former heroin addict turned to Christ, a New York garment tycoon, a male sociologist gone registered nurse—hospitality and intimate conversations came easy, and lone strangers shared lives.

Ten days later I was dropped off at Parry Sound, Ontario on the rocky Georgian Bay. And the incredible variety of people I'd brushed lives with had shown me something about the Unification Church. This "world-saving" organization, with its strict and narrow definitions of how life should be lived and what a man should be, probably could not tolerate, much less incorporate the many different peoples of the earth and their many beautiful and very human idiosyncracies.

In my Canadian woods retreat I felt suddenly freed from my obsession with defending my Unification faith and criticizing "the opposition." My massive 500-page log turned into a clearinghouse for my Unification Church experience. As I recorded the entire three-and-a-half-year saga, old hurts, doubts, joys, inspirations and disillusionments flowed freely onto the pages and stared me in the face. My August 24 entry reads: "I remember times in the Unification Church when my love for Jesus was greater than my love for the 'True Parents'; more profound and deeply touching. And now my love for Jesus Christ and His words is stronger still. But compared to Jesus Christ, Sun Myung Moon is supposed to be like the Sun compared to a lightbulb and it is supposed to be much easier to love and develop a deep 'spiritual connection' with the True Parents than it is with Jesus!" That's funny. That hasn't been my experience.

> August 26, 1977
>   . . . "Why in two years you'll be a world leader!" Daniel had retorted. . . . Everyone, including the leaders, expects a big breakthrough any year where great numbers of people will swarm to Unification Church centers to sign up. . . . It is also a common U.C. delusion that by the year 2000 the majority of the world will believe in the "Divine Principle" and the True Parents. I know for myself that this was one of my greatest hopes. . . . A delusion! . . . The whole darn Unification Church family is suffering under this *mass delusion* of "any year now," imminent glory and victory! Sorry Charlie. No way. When it happens I'll be there fast to check it out.

I began wondering what I'd be doing 30 years from now if I stuck with the movement. Maybe *then* the world wouldn't, as we'd all believed, be well on its way towards affluence and perfection. Perhaps I'd be a clerk in a movement warehouse, grounded with no skills and no education, in a world which still considered the Unification Church a small, aberrant cult.

And 1981! That monumental date—the last year of Sun Myung Moon's 21-year course (styled after "Jacob's Course") which began in 1960 with the wedding of the "True Parents." 1981! The year marking the "establishment of the foundation of the kingdom of heaven."

In 1974 Fred Seymour and I agreed: "1981! That's only seven years away. *I'm* willing to wait till '81 to see whether all this really happens!" Well, I was beginning to suspect that when 1981 rolled around nothing much would have changed. "Father" would proclaim that some sort of "foundation of the kingdom of heaven" had been established, and then he'd give us another five-, or seven-year plan to get excited about.*

August 27, 1977
   From my own experience I know that the latent talents, creativity and individual expression of many members is stifled in the Unification Church. . . . After two years in the "Family," "world leader" was a farcical term for the depressed and uninspired fundraiser I had become. Of course if a U.C. member were reading this he'd think, "But, we're going to the bottom of hell to pay indemnity to restore our ancestors and six thousand years of fallen history, and we must accept it with a *grateful heart!*"
   Well that's how I rationalized all the suffering and states of psychological depression Unification Church members go through. But I don't buy that rationalization anymore. Yes, I do believe there is some aspect of trial, of having to "carry one's cross," for anyone who's desiring to know and live for God. . . . But one must make a distinction between this and the kind of malaise or depressed, *joyless* state so many Church members live under.

I began reading Robert J. Lifton's *Thought Reform and the Psychology of Totalism*, as well as other books on mind control and coercive persuasion. Dr. Lifton is professor of psychology at Yale University and studied Chinese Communist brainwashing. Chapter 22 suggests a set of eight criteria, eight psychological themes, predominant in ideological totalism and "against which any environment may be judged—a basis for answering the ever-recurring question: 'Isn't this just like brainwashing?' "[28]

When I read Chapter 22 I whooped inside and streaked my pen underneath almost every other line. It seemed Lifton had worked out the eight criteria of Moon's Unification Church!

---

* True to form, in 1980 Moon gave his followers another carrot on a stick by declaring that America must be saved by 1987!

August 30, 1977

. . . These books did help me to see my Unification Church experience in a new light. . . . The very nature of ideological totalism is negative and destructive to the development of creative ability and human potential. Therefore I must ask, "Is the Unification Church a 'totalist' organization?" More and more I'm having to admit to myself that it is.

. . . As I ponder this question there are some helpful thoughts which come to mind. . . . Could a religion be a true religion if it dictated every aspect of life, an absolute standard concerning how one should live? Could not such a "total" definition of what human life should be end up hampering the development of man rather than "eliminating the evil" in him, rather than realizing the "true man"?

What it comes down to is this: . . . how far can a religion go in the direction to totalism before it becomes so constricting and absolute that it takes away the very joy and richness of human life it is attempting to bring about? How far can a religion go in this direction before it ceases to be a true religion?

Then I began perusing my Carriage House study session notes. A statement by Dr. Swope looked out at me from the page—"In the cults, human decency and welfare are sacrificed in striving for the higher purpose." This I could no longer deny. And the violations were many; to name a few:

1. Practicing deception in recruiting
2. Trespassing, misrepresentation and fraud in fund-raising
3. Soliciting without permits
4. Registering one or two persons in a motel room and cramming in a whole team
5. Taking advantage of human sympathy by fund-raising in wheel chairs
6. Dangerously ignoring members' medical needs.

Since my "rescue" I'd never seriously questioned Sun Myung Moon's moral character because I'd wanted to stay as "impartial" as possible. Now I let the doubts run free like squirrels from a cage. I'd never been able to get it straight whether Sun Myung Moon had been married two times or three times (or more). And I'd never liked "Father's" plans for buying the Empire State Building. The idea was mainly a publicity venture so that, as one high Korean member put it, "Whenever people see the Empire State Building, they'll think of Reverend Moon!" The whole scheme smacked of megalomania and I'd wondered why "Father" couldn't instead use some of his money to really *help* people. On August 30 I recorded in my log,

"Still have strong feelings of loyalty towards the Unification Church.

> September 1, 1977
> Early yesterday morning I packed up my campsite
> and bade farewell to beautiful Parry Sound. She had
> been good to me (only one downpour).

I hitched south to Toronto and spent the entire day trying to track down Gary Johnson. He'd moved out of his apartment and left no forwarding address. And calling every "G. Johnson" in the Toronto phonebook had failed to flush him out.

In the evening I poked around the campus of the University of Toronto and found a lovely monkish chapel in the Hart House (the student activities building).

> September 1, 1977
> . . . I entered the chapel in a very distraught and
> unhappy mood. The Divine Principle "Mission of
> Jesus" was bothering me again. I just can't get that
> interpretation of Christ's mission out of my head.

[Namely that Jesus essentially failed His mission and achieved little: only limited salvation for mankind. This haunting belief would swallow up my excitement and joy about the Christian faith and leave me with a vision of a crucified Man who may have died for little or nothing.]

> After praying. . . I cried deeply, asking for God's guid-
> ance. Then I read Jesus' Sermon on the Mount. It
> inspired me as it always does. . . . These are hard
> times, man, real hard times.
> Afterwards I felt deeply comforted and experienced

a peace and a love I know was from God. I stayed another hour in the chapel and prayed. It just flowed forth—a communion of love.

I watched as the white-helmeted figure motorcycled across the campus of London's University of Western Ontario and turned onto the plaza. It was Gary Johnson. By some strange turn of events I had been able to contact Gary's parents and then locate him at a farm 20 miles west of London.

After he parked his bike we grasped hands and then embraced. I couldn't remember the last time I'd been so happy to see a fellow human being. Gary was 27 now, a senior engineering student, with a handsome beard and full head of blonde hair. But he still looked like the Gary I'd known in Berkeley and on the New England IOWC, the Gary I'd always respected as a level-headed older brother.

And we talked. All day long we talked and talked—on the plaza, in the cafeteria, on the road, and in the quiet of the old farmhouse. It was so good to open up to someone in complete honesty for the first time in five months! All that time I'd wrestled inside a world of fear, guilt, anger and doubt, a world I would not and could not share with anyone.

As I poured out my story I listened intently to Gary's account of why he'd left the Unification Church. Minute by minute, point by point, the key disillusionments which had caused Gary to leave the group closely or precisely matched many arguments I had heard at the Carriage House.

Gary had always felt uneasy about the way we misrepresented ourselves in both fund-raising and recruiting. He also found the Unification Church totally obsessed with moneymaking. At times it had made Gary sick to see Sun Myung Moon and high Church officials living in comfort and luxury when so many members had nothing.

After a steaming rice and vegetable dinner Gary thumped his mug of coffee down on the kitchen table. "And there was this 'Master Speaks' which says that we should have Sun Myung Moon's name branded on our heads and hands. It scared me because it seemed so violent and reminded me of prophecies in Revelation about the 'mark of the beast.'"

And that night, with hot coffee, pleasant kitchen shadows

and crickets in the yard, Gary related his encounters with Jesus Christ and Christianity and how He had been the most important factor in his leaving the movement. At the 1974 Madison Square Garden rally a Christian had handed Gary a leaflet. He opened it and read: "Reverend Moon can't save you," and the reasons why not. His faith was deeply shaken.

After he returned to Boston he spent an evening at a Christian church's presentation of a film portraying what the end times might be like. He remembered the title as "Unity"; and towards the end of the film the landscape had swarmed with Dodge vans bearing the slogan "UNITE!"

Though Gary didn't exactly agree with the movie's interpretation of Revelation, he left that night very shaken with doubts—"Am I doing the right thing? Am I really doing the right thing?"

And Gary then prayed to Jesus that He either show him whether the Unification Church was true, *or* draw him out of the group if it was false. In the following 11 months before Gary left the movement, he repeated this prayer many times. For this reason Gary believed that it was Jesus Christ who drew him out of the Unification Church.

And how was Gary Johnson doing now? He was by no means spiritually dead nor cut off and abandoned by God as ex-members were supposed to be. Rather, Gary confirmed a secret hope that a man could lead a *personal* and also *public* life founded solidly in a relationship with God. Gary enjoyed free time and also actively participated in and contributed to the world as a budding solar engineer. And his life's foundation was a deep faith in a spiritual reality: his God, his Lord Jesus Christ. His faith was not perpetuated by group or self-indoctrination, but was rather a confident, intelligent faith rooted in critical thought, concerned prayer, study and understanding.

It was midnight: Gary and I were lounging in the dark living room of the farmhouse: The stereo poured out a soothing Cat Stevens tune, "Father and Son." A candle on the coffee table flickered and cast dancing shadows on the walls. I lay embraced in an old stuffed armchair, staring into the candle flame.

And just as a dying man sees his entire life flash before him, a panoramic view of three-and-a-half years in Sun Myung Moon's Unification Church film-reeled in my thoughts. Three-and-a-half years of following a way I'd deeply and sincerely believed was true and right. We'd been one family striving to build a new world. We'd fought so hard and suffered so much.

But then followed the Carriage House and my recent journey. And the whole experience had been like coming down off a drug. Dulled senses and feelings and a warped perception of life and the world had become clear, vibrant, and poignant. Now the last merciless holds on my mind were peeling away and clattering to the earth like defeated chains.

The list of doubts, discrepancies and violations was already *much* too long—and Gary's testimony came as the straw that broke the camel's back. No longer could I in good conscience and conviction continue to be a part of the Unification Church. In fact there wasn't a snowman's chance in hell that Sun Myung Moon was the Messiah.

As the music swept over my spirit large teardrops began to roll down my cheeks, tears of great unburdening. Gary was lying half-asleep on the couch. "Hey, Gary, you know what?"

"No, what?" mumbled Gary.

"I'm never going back . . . I'm never going back . . . never, never, *never.*"

Then I broke down and cried for a good long beautiful minute.

At last I was free.

Epilogue

*"So if the Son makes you free,
you will be free indeed,"*
John 8:36

The next morning I *jumped* out of bed for the first time in years. Through my second floor window I watched a red, shimmering disk cut the horizon beyond the barns, misty pastures and woods. The sun is beautiful. Why hadn't I realized it before? Then I noticed that the nausea and nagging fear were completely gone. *Gone!* Truly, freedom had replaced bondage. And that day I couldn't help but roar through the fields and meadows—leaping into blue space, clicking my heels and bellowing, "I'm free! . . . I'm free! . . . I'm freeeeeeee!"

I felt like an eagle who'd long been caged, grown tired and stale, but was then released into the morning sun before the finish of his youth. I was soaring to heights I had never known. I was liberated from the fear, from the burden of having to save the world. My mind had broken free from the prison of that cold, absolute ideology which had robbed my world of its mysteries and complexities, my life of its richness and joy.

I stayed at the farm with Gary and Tony and Jan Zaplatter, working hard to shake off the remaining lies and distortions of Moonism. Bible study and some consulting with theologians at the University of Toronto further exposed in the *Divine Principle* a twisted and erroneous interpretation of the Old and New Testaments and the mission of Jesus. Bible verses are often quoted out of context and given twisted meanings. For example, John 16:13 and Luke 17:25 are two quotations crucial to the "Divine Principle" which, when closely examined, clearly *do not* refer to "the Lord of the Second Advent" but rather to the Holy Spirit and Jesus.

And with the help of a distinguished Old Testament scholar, Dr. S.D. Walters of Knox College at the University of Toronto, I discovered that many historical periods in Moon's history parallels are grossly inaccurate or fabricated. Sometimes I was totally flabbergasted at how much I and everyone in the Unification Church had been deceived.

Though it took a while to figure out, it finally dawned on me that I'd never freely and consciously *chosen* to follow Sun Myung Moon. At a vulnerable time in my life I'd stumbled into a system that by deception, mind manipulation, and manipulation by fear and guilt, can deftly funnel the young and idealistic into following its Messiah. Clearly, the element of free choice does not play a role here.

During my four-week Ontario-farm retreat I continued my investigation of Christianity. I was overjoyed that in disavowing the religious cult of Sun Myung Moon, I didn't also have to disavow and discard all sincere spiritual and religious pursuits. I realized that a person can leave a religious cult and still pursue a meaningful relationship with God, still gather with others in sharing his faith and his search for God.

On the other hand, parts of me cautioned against jumping from one frying pan into another. But in the course of sorting things out I realized that Christianity was not another cult into which I was rebounding. The Christian faith had drawn my mind out of the Moon-cult's grip. And the energizing relationship with God which had emerged during my last year in the group and at the Carriage House was *not* a product of my having lived by the "Divine Principle" or of my having followed Sun Myung Moon, but rather a result of my encounters with real Christianity and with Jesus. In fact, now the chains and entrapments of Moonism had almost completely fallen away, leaving me only one step away from becoming a Christian.

Probably the greatest hindrance in making that one last step and embracing Christianity was the concept of indemnity. According to this Unification principle, salvation equals spiritual perfection (total oneness with God) which can only be achieved by a man's constant 100 percent effort in both faith and action. Christianity on the other hand teaches that God's salvation is a *gift*. Dr. Swope had once appropriately explained this concept, "The main point of Christianity which is not in any other religion is that we come to salvation only by God's graciousness, not by our doing, not by our works."[29]

I began reevaluating the indemnity concept and found myself tired of feeling that God was keeping a scorecard, that the quality of my relationship with God depended on how much indemnity I'd paid. Most of all, I was tired of not feeling that I'd finally and forever come home to the heavenly Father. In the Unification Church there had never been true peace or "rightness" with God.

What finally convinced me that the principle of indemnity was false was an examination of my own experience in the group. For three-and-a-half years I'd sacrificed everything, paid enough indemnity to kill a horse. Yet, in terms of my spiritual growth, namely a closing or shrinking of the chasm between God and myself, all this indemnity, this mountain of works, had gotten me *nowhere.* It seemed that indemnity placed overbearing emphasis on works and suffering rather than on acting out of love for and faith in God, and therefore could not bring one significantly closer to the heavenly Father.

Finally, the idea that God's salvation was a gift, a concept that I had on occasion ridiculed as absurdly simple, even unfair and foolish, was the only thing that made any sense, the only covenant between God and man which seemed capable of transcending the abyss between Creator and created.

Although I'd had trouble accepting that salvation was a gift, I had no trouble accepting that it had been accomplished by Jesus Christ's death and resurrection. No problem. The imposter-Messiah had been dumped, along with his lie that Jesus had failed to accomplish full redemption. I already admired and loved this person who in recent months had become my "Main-Man," the example for my life. After three-and-a-half years in a movement which scorned His salvation I could accept Jesus Christ joyfully and say with the doubting Thomas, "My Lord and my God!"

Three-and-a-half years have passed since I found my freedom; and they've been the happiest years of my life. In October, 1977 I left Gary and hitchhiked to Austin, Texas to be with my parents. Having finally realized what they had done for me, what incredible anguish they had endured, I could embrace them in gratitude and inexpressible love. I now love them more than ever and we are very close.

In 1978—joy and victory. I returned to college at the University of Michigan in Ann Arbor. It was like scrambling up and over that high ridge I'd once thought unattainable, and then passing into the valley of my dreams. Some aspects of readjusting to the world outside the cult have been painful and difficult; but mostly I've experienced great excitement, inspiration and joy in my rediscovering of life and the world, and I feel I've grown and matured in my personal and spiritual life.

Although I was not harassed by the Moonies as some ex-members have been, for over a year I received letters and phone calls from old "Brothers and Sisters" like Mike Chapman and Arlane. Now I realize that I'll never forget these friends on "the other side." Though I believe that the Moon-cult as a whole is destructive and dangerous, I feel only love and empathy for individual members of the Unification Church. The young people I came to know during those years are good people, *very* good people—individuals with magnanimous hope, energy, sincerity, and dedication to things great and good. I'll never forget them.

Yet Unification Church members are also victims of mental, psychological and spiritual bondage. Though they perceive themselves as representing the new Messiah, in reality they represent beautiful people whose lives are being tragically wasted. If I have any message of hope for current Unification Church members and all members of today's cults, it is this: the "outside world" is *not* devoid of God, is *not* devoid of love. God is alive and well and living amongst the many peoples of the earth. There are former group members, family and friends who love, care and pray for them, and who are anxious to speak with and help them in any way possible. This is my message, my hope for my brothers and sisters in the cults, that they may know and realize these things, and perhaps someday find their freedom.

October 27, 1977
I'm free. . . . I can live again. Sit back on a bean

bag, a couch and relax and look around me and think. Time to think, to relish thoughts, dreams and hopes that reach out far, many years into the future. Where before in the Unification Church there was only darkness and void when I looked into the future, now I see horizons stretching bright in the morning sun. I can have a free experience of the living God without any group; take advantage of life's exciting possibilities and options; and take part in a free development of my individual self. And I can love again, express love I could not express before!

I'm free now. Free! 10,000 times I must have screamed it in the fields and on the highways, whispered it to the setting sun and to the night as I lay in bed, proclaimed it to my dear mother and father and friends who had thought that I was lost forever. I'm free.

An Appeal

In the United States alone, cults number between 2,500 and 5,000 and involve two to three million young adults as members. We can take action to help cult victims and to protect others from falling prey to the cult groups, whether it be the Unification Church, Scientology or another Jim Jones' Peoples Temple. The following are a few suggestions in this regard.

1. High school and college young people must be informed about the cults and how they operate. Many churches and schools have already established cult information programs. Still, many more are needed.

2. Without endangering other rights, we can and must enact legislation which will discourage deception and fraud in both fund-raising and recruiting by the cults.

3. We must create and support groups which practice sensitive, tender and loving rehabilitation of cult victims.

4. Finally, Christians and Christian churches must get their act together by trying to meet the spiritual needs of young people, all people—nurturing intelligent and deep faith, practicing the words of love. "I was hungry and you gave me food, . . . I was a stranger and you welcomed me, . . . [insofar] as you did it to one of the least of these my brethren, you did it to me" (see Matt. 25:35,40).

Inasmuch as we practice Jesus' words there will be love and caring. And where there is love and caring, the magnetism and power of the cults will be rendered ineffective.

Notes

1. Sun Myung Moon, "The Significance of the Training Session," "The Master Speaks," May 17, 1972.
2. Jean Merritt, "Open Letter," 1975.
3. "Gonna Build a Kingdom," paraphrased. The Unification Church.
4. Ibid.
5. "Moon Shadow" by Cat Stevens, 1970. Used by permission.
6. Commandant, POW camp in Korea, 1954. Quoted in a British chaplain's account of his imprisonment, E.H. Schein, *Coercial Persuasion.* Appeared originally in S.Jhe Oakland-Berkeley Family.
7. The Unification Pledge Card
8. Notes taken by author at a talk given by Onni to Oakland-Berkeley Family.
9. Ibid.
10. "Day of Hope," paraphrased. The Unification Church.
11. "Sun Myung Moon, a Biography," a leaflet published by the Unification Church in Berkeley, California, p. 2.
12. Kwan Yol Yoo, "The Church's Birth in Pusan," *New Hope News,* 28 August, 1974, p. 24.
13. Jane Day Mook, "The Unification Church," A.D., May 1974, p. 34.
14. Sun Myung Moon, "The Future of Christianity," Christianity in Crisis (Washington D.C.: Holy Spirit Association-Unification World Christianity HSA-UWC, Inc., 1974), p. 114.
15. Ibid., p. 114.
16. Sun Myung Moon, "The Way of God's Will," a collection of aphorisms translated from the Japanese, #46.
17. Sun Myung Moon, "Parent's Day," The Master Speaks MS-46, 24 March, 1974.
18. Jerry Carrol, "Moon's Plan to Stop Communism," *San Francisco Chronicle,* December 10, 1975.
19. John Cotter, "Rev. Moon Seeks Power Through 'Gospel,' " *Chicago Tribune,* De-

cember 14, 1975, p. 12.

20. 1977-78 Report of the House Foreign Affairs Subcommittee Investigation into Korean-American Relations.

21. John Cotter, p. 1; and "Parent's Day," p. 9.

22. From notes taken by author during Sun Myung Moon's speech to the MFT, October, 1975 at Upshur House in Washington D.C.

23. From notes taken by author during Sun Myung Moon's speech at the Belvedere estate on Sunday, May 30, 1976.

24. Malcolm Muggeridge, *Something Beautiful for God* (Garden City, NY: Double-day and Company, Inc., 1977), p. 53.

25. Ibid.

26. "For Those Tears I Died" by Martha J. Stevens. © 1969 by Lexicon Music, Inc. ASCAP. All rights reserved. International copyright secured. Used by permission.

27. "Let It Shine," paraphrased. The Unification church.

28. Robert Jay Lifton, M.D., *Thought Reform and the Psychology of Totalism—A Study of "Brainwashing" in China* (New York: W.W. Norton, 1963), p. 420.

29. Dr. George Swope, "Kids and Cults—Who Joins and Why," *Media and Methods,* May/June 1980.